Service Strategy based on ITIL ®

Other publications by Van Haren Publishing

Van Haren Publishing (VHP) specializes in titles on Best Practices, methods and standards within IT management, Architecture (Enterprise and IT), business management and project management.

These publications are grouped in series, eg: *ITSM Library* (on behalf of ITSMF International), *Best Practice* and *IT Management Topics*. VHP is also publisher on behalf of leading companies and institutions, eg The Open Group, IPMA-NL, CA, Getronics, Pink Elephant. At the time of going to press the following books are available:

IT (Service) Management / IT Governance
ITSM, ITIL® V3 and ITIL® V2
Foundations of IT Service Management – based on ITIL® V3 (English, Dutch, German; French, Japanese and Spanish editions)
Introduction to IT Service Management (ITIL V3, English)
IT Service Management based on ITIL V3 – A Pocket Guide (English, Dutch, German, Italian; French, Japanese and Spanish editions)
Foundations of IT Service Management based on ITIL® (ITIL V2), (English, Dutch, French, German, Spanish, Japanese, Chinese, Danish, Italian, Korean, Russian, Arabic)
Implementing Service and Support Management Processes (English)
Release and Control for IT Service Management, based on ITIL® – A Practitioner Guide (English)

ISO/IEC 20000
ISO/IEC 20000 – An Introduction (English, German)
Implementing ISO/IEC 20000 Certification (English)
ISO/IEC 20000 – A Pocket Guide (English, Italian, German, Spanish, Portuguese)

ISO 27001 and ISO 17799
Information Security based on ISO 27001 and ISO 17799 – A Management Guide (English)
Implementing Information Security based on ISO 27001 and ISO 17799 – A Management Guide (English)

COBIT
IT Governance based on COBIT4.1® – A Management Guide (English, German, Japanese)

IT Service CMM
IT Service CMM – A Pocket Guide (English)

ASL and BiSL
ASL – A Framework for Application Management (English, German)
ASL – Application Services Library – A Management Guide (English, Dutch)
BiSL – A Framework for Business Information Management (Dutch, English)
BiSL – Business information Services Library – A Management Guide (Dutch; English)

ISPL
IT Services Procurement op basis van ISPL (Dutch)
IT Services Procurement based on ISPL – A Pocket Guide (English)

Other IT Management titles:
De RfP voor IT-outsourcing (Dutch; English version due Spring 2008)
Decision- en Controlfactoren voor IT-Sourcing (Dutch)
Defining IT Success through the Service Catalogue (English)
Frameworks for IT Management – An introduction (English, Japanese; German)
Frameworks for IT Management – A Pocket Guide (English, German, Dutch)
Implementing IT Governance (English)
Implementing leading standards for IT management (English, Dutch)
IT Service Management global best practices, volume 1 (English)
IT Service Management Best Practices, volume 1, 2, 3 and 4 (Dutch)
ITSM from hell! / ITSM from hell based on Not ITIL (English)
ITSMP – The IT Strategy Management Process (English)

Metrics for IT Service Management (English, Russian)
Service Management Process Maps (English)
Six Sigma for IT Management (English)
Six Sigma for IT Management – A Pocket Guide (English)

MOF/MSF
MOF – Microsoft Operations Framework, A Pocket Guide (Dutch, English, French, German, Japanese)
MSF – Microsoft Solutions Framework, A Pocket Guide (English, German)

Architecture (Enterprise and IT)
TOGAF, The Open Group Architecture Framework – A Management Guide (English)
The Open Group Architecture Framework – 2007 Edition (English, official publication of TOG)
TOGAF™ Version 8 Enterprise Edition – Study Guide (English, official publication of TOG)
TOGAF™ Version 8.1.1 Enterprise Edition –A Pocket Guide (English, official publication of TOG)

Business Management
ISO 9000
ISO 9001:2000 – The Quality Management Process (English)

EFQM
The EFQM excellence model for Assessing Organizational Performance – A Management Guide (English)

SqEME®
Process management based on SqEME® (English)
SqEME® – A Pocket Guide (English, Dutch)

Project/Programme/Risk Management
ICB/NCB
NCB Versie 3– Nederlandse Competence Baseline (Dutch, on behalf of IPMA-NL)
Projectmanagement op basis van NCB V3 – IPMA-C en IPMA-D (Dutch)

PRINCE2™
Project Management based on PRINCE2™– Edition 2005 (English, Dutch, German)
PRINCE2™ – A No Nonsense Management Guide (English)
PRINCE2™ voor opdrachtgevers – Management Guide (Dutch)

MINCE®
MINCE® – A Framework for Organizational Maturity (English)

MSP
Programme Management based on MSP (English, Dutch)
Programme Management based on MSP – A Management Guide (English)

M_o_R
Risk Management based on M_o_R – A Management Guide (English)

Other publications on project management:
Wegwijzer voor methoden bij Projectvolwassenheid (Dutch: fall 2008)
Het Project Management Office – Management Guide (Dutch)

For the latest information on VHP publications, visit our website: www.vanharen.net

Service Strategy
based on ITIL® V3

A Management Guide

Van Haren
PUBLISHING

Colophon

Title:	Service Strategy based on ITIL® V3 - A Management Guide
Authors:	Jan van Bon (Chief Editor, Inform-IT)
	Arjen de Jong (co-author, Inform-IT)
	Axel Kolthof (co-author, Inform-IT)
	Mike Pieper (co-author, Inform-IT)
	Ruby Tjassing (co-author, Inform-IT)
	Annelies van der Veen (co-author, Inform-IT)
	Tieneke Verheijen (co-author, Inform-IT)
Copy editor:	Jayne Wilkinson
Publisher:	Van Haren Publishing, Zaltbommel, www.vanharen.net
Design & layout:	CO2 Premedia bv, Amersfoort - NL
ISBN:	9789087531249
Edition:	First edition, first impression, June 2008

Foreword

ITIL receives more and more attention on a global scale, with many companies adopting its principles. In that respect, ITIL version 2 has done a good job. The update of ITIL in version 3, released in June 2007, has caused some concern for many of these companies, since it built on the idea that companies had already achieved results with version 2 content. In practice however, most companies are still working their way through the basic principles of ITIL. For that reason, the "Foundations of IT Service Management - based on ITIL V3" was developed, offering a comprehensive but easy-to-understand source of information on ITIL. This title is now widely used as the authoritative guide on ITIL V3 in training situations and in implementations.

Apart from offering the market a summarized, easy-to-understand source on ITIL V3, that can be used for a step-by-step approach, many companies focus on a subset of the ITIL best practices. That is why we developed a series of ITIL Management Guides, focusing on the processes, procedures, and functions, from each of the phases of the ITIL V3 Lifecycle. This enables companies to focus on those phases that are of primary concern to them.

Each of the five ITIL V3 Management Guides is structured the same way as the successful Foundations book: it separates the Lifecycle information from the single process, procedure and function components, enabling organizations to take their own approach and still adopt ITIL best practices.

The content of each guide was derived from the Foundations book, which ensures that you'll find the same high quality as usual. This means that all content has been peer-reviewed in a rigorous way, making sure that it completely aligns to ITIL V3, but also that it was the best, concise and comprehensive summary of ITIL V3 core content that could be achieved.

I'm convinced that this new management guide will provide an excellent reference tool for practitioners, students and others who want to have a practical guide on the key ITIL V3 concepts.

Jan van Bon

Chief Editor

Acknowledgements

This Management Guide is a compilation of the itSMF publication "Foundations of IT Service Management - Based on ITIL V3". Thus, the international review team that reviewed "Foundations of IT Service Management", has contributed indirectly to this Management Guide. We would like to thank all reviewers once again for their detailed review which improved the quality of both books significantly.

The review team consists of:
- John van Beem, ISES International, Netherlands
- Aad Brinkman, Apreton, Netherlands
- Peter Brooks, PHMB Consulting, itSMF South Africa
- Rob van der Burg, Microsoft, Netherlands
- Judith Cremers, Getronics PinkRoccade Educational Services, Netherlands
- Robert Falkowitz, Concentric Circle Consulting, itSMF Switzerland
- Rosario Fondacaro, Quint Wellington Redwood, Italy
- Peter van Gijn, LogicaCMG, Netherlands
- Jan Heunks, ICT Partners, Netherlands
- Linh Ho, Compuware Corporation, USA
- Ton van der Hoogen, ToTZ Diensten, Netherlands
- Kevin Holland, NHS, UK
- Matiss Horodishtiano, Amdocs, itSMF Israel
- Wim Hoving, BHVB, Netherlands
- Brian Johnson, CA, USA
- Georges Kemmerling, Quint Wellington Redwood, Netherlands
- Kirstie Magowan, itSMF New Zealand
- Steve Mann, OpSys - SM2, itSMF Belgium
- Reiko Morita, Ability InterBusiness Solutions, Inc., Japan
- Jürgen Müller, Marval Benelux, Netherlands
- Ingrid Ouwerkerk, Getronics PinkRoccade Educational Services, Netherlands
- Ton Sleutjes, CapGemini, Netherlands
- Maxime Sottini, Innovative Consulting, itSMF Italy
- Takashi Yagi, Hitachi Ltd., itSMF Japan

Given the desire for a broad consensus in the IT Service Management field, new developments, additional material and contributions from ITSM professionals who have worked with ITIL version 3 are welcome. They will be discussed by the editors and where appropriate incorporated into new editions. Comments can be sent to the Chief Editor, Jan van Bon, email: j.van.bon@inform-it.org.

Contents

Introduction

1.1 Background

Developments in IT have had a tremendous effect on the business market during the last decade. Since the appearance of extremely powerful hardware, highly versatile software and super-fast networks, all connected to each other worldwide, organizations have been able to develop their information-dependent products and services to a greater extent, and to bring them to the market much faster. These developments have marked the transition of the industrial age into the **information age**. In the information age, everything has become faster and more dynamic, and everything is connected.

Traditional hierarchical organizations often have difficulties in responding to this rapidly changing market, and this has led to current trends for organizations to become flatter and more flexible. The focus has shifted from vertical silos to horizontal **processes**, and decision-making powers are increasingly bestowed on the employees. It is against this background that the work processes of IT service management have arisen.

An important advantage of process-oriented organizations is that processes can be designed to support a **customer-oriented approach**. This has made the alignment between the IT organization (responsible for supplying information) and the customer (responsible for using these information systems in their business) increasingly significant. Over the last couple of years, this trend has attracted attention under the title of **Business-IT Alignment (BITA)**.

As organizations gained more experience with the **process-oriented approach** of IT service management, it became clear that the process must be managed coherently.

Furthermore, it was obvious that the introduction of a process-oriented work method meant a big change for the primarily line and project-oriented organizations. Culture and change management proved to be crucial elements for a successful organizational design.

Another important lesson learned was that the IT organization must not lose itself in a process culture. Just like the one-sided project-oriented organization, a one-sided process-oriented organization was not the optimum type of business. Balance was, as always, the magic word. In addition, it became clear that the customer-oriented approach required that an **end-to-end** and **user-centric** approach must be followed: it was of no help to the user to know that "the server was still in operation" if the information system was not available at the user's workplace. IT services must be viewed in a larger context. The need for the recognition of the **Service Lifecycle**, and the management of IT services in light of that lifecycle, became a concern.

Due to the fast growing dependency of business upon information, the quality of information services in companies is being increasingly subjected to stricter **internal and external requirements**. The role of **standards** is getting more and more important, and **frameworks** of "best practices" help with the development of a management system to meet these requirements. Organizations that are not in control of their processes, will not be able to realize great results on the level of the Service Lifecycle and the end-to-end-management of those services. Organizations that do not have their internal organization in order, will also not achieve great results. For these reasons, all these aspects are handled alongside each other in the course of this book.

1.2 Why this book

This book offers detailed information for those who are responsible for strategic information issues, as well as for the (much larger) group who are responsible for setting up and executing the delivery of the information systems. This is supported by both the description of the Service Lifecycle, as documented in ITIL version 3, and by the description of the processes that are associated with it. The ITIL core books are very extensive, and can be used for a thorough study of contemporary best practices. This management guide provides the reader with an easy-to-read comprehensive introduction to the broad library of ITIL core books, to support the understanding and the further distribution of ITIL as an industry standard. Once this understanding of the structure of ITIL has been gained, the reader can use the core books for a more detailed understanding and guidance for their daily practice.

1.3 Organizations

Several organizations are involved in the maintenance of ITIL as a description of the "best practice" in the IT service management field.

OGC

Initially ITIL was a product of the CCTA, a UK Government Organization. On 1 April 2001 the CCTA was incorporated into the OGC, which thus became the new owner of ITIL. The aim of the OGC is to help its clients (within the UK Government) with the modernization of their procurement activities and the improvement of their services, by, among other things, making the best possible use of IT: "OGC aims to modernize procurement in government, and deliver substantial value for money improvements". The OGC promotes the use of "best practices" in numerous areas, such as project management, program management, procurement, risk management and IT service management. For this reason the OGC itself has published several series of books (Libraries) which have been written by (international) experts from different companies and organizations.

itSMF

The target group for this publication is anyone who is involved or interested in IT service management. A professional organization, working on the development of the IT service management field, has been created especially for this target group.

In 1991 the Information Technology Service Management Forum (itSMF), originally known as the Information Technology Infrastructure Management Forum (ITIMF), was set up as a UK association. In 1994, a sister-association was established in the Netherlands, following the UK example.

Since then, independent itSMF organizations have been set up in more than forty countries, spread across the globe, and the number of "chapters" continues to grow. All itSMF organizations operate under the umbrella organization, itSMF International (itSMF-I).

itSMF is aimed at the entire professional area of IT service management. It promotes the exchange of information and experiences that IT organizations can use to improve their service provision. itSMF is also involved in the use and quality of the various standards and methods that are important in the field. One of these standards is ITIL. and itSMF International has an agreement with OGC and APM Group on the promotion of the use of ITIL.

APM Group

In 2006, OGC contracted the management of ITIL rights, the certification of ITIL exams and accreditation of training organizations to the APM Group (APMG), a commercial organization. APMG defines the certification and accreditation for the ITIL exams, and published the new certification system (see Section 2.1: ITIL exams).

Exam bodies

The Dutch foundation Examen Instituut voor Informatica (EXIN) and the English Information Systems Examination Board (ISEB, part of the BCS: the British Computer Society) cooperated in the development and provision of certification for IT service management. For many years they were the only bodies that provided ITIL exams. With the contracting of APMG by OGC, the responsibility for ITIL exams is now with APMG. To support the world-wide delivery of these ITIL exams, APMG has accredited a number of exam bodies: EXIN, BCS/ISEB, and Loyalist College, Canada.

1.4   Structure of the book

Chapter 2, introduces the Service Lifecycle, in the context of IT service management and IT governance. It discusses principles of organizational maturity, and the benefits and risks of following a service management framework. This chapter ends with the introduction of the Service Lifecycle.

In Chapters 3 the Service Strategy lifecycle phase is discussed in detail, in a standardized structure.

Chapter 4 provides general information on principles of processes, teams, roles, functions, positions, tools, and other elements of interest.

In chapter 5, the processes and functions of Service Strategy are described in detail. Each of these processes and functions is described in terms of:
- Introduction
- Activities, methods and techniques
- Interfaces, inputs and outputs
- Metrics and Key Performance Indicators (KPIs)
- Implementation, with Critical Success Factors (CSFs), challenges, risks and traps

The appendices provide useful sources for the reader. A reference list of used sources is provided, as well as the official ITIL Glossary and a list with acronyms. The book ends with an extensive index of relevant terms that will support the reader in finding relevant text elements.

CHAPTER 2

Introduction to the Service Lifecycle

2.1 Introduction to ITIL

In the 1980s the quality of service provided by both internal and external IT companies to UK government departments was of such a level that the CCTA (Central Computer and Telecommunications Agency, now the Office of Government Commerce, OGC) was instructed by the Government to develop a standard approach for an efficient and effective delivery of IT services. This was to be an approach which was independent of the suppliers (whether internal or external). The result of this instruction was the development and publication of the **Information Technology Infrastructure Library™** (ITIL). ITIL is made up of a collection of "best practices" found across the range of IT service providers.

ITIL offers a systematic approach to the delivery of quality of IT services. It gives a detailed description of most of the important processes in an IT organization, and includes checklists for tasks, procedures and responsibilities which can be used as a basis for tailoring to the needs of individual organizations.

At the same time, the broad coverage of ITIL also provides a helpful reference guide for many areas, which can be used to develop new improvement goals for an IT organization, enabling it to grow and mature.

Over the years, ITIL has become much more than a series of useful books about IT service management. The framework for the "best practice" in IT service management is promoted and further developed by advisors, trainers and suppliers of technologies or products. Since the nineties, ITIL represents not only the theoretical framework, but the approach and philosophy shared by the people who work with it in practice.

Being an extended framework of best practices for IT service management itself, the advantages and disadvantages of frameworks in general, described in Section 2.5, are also applicable to ITIL. Of course, ITIL was developed because of the advantages mentioned earlier. Many of the pointers from "best practices" are intended to avoid potential problems, or, should they occur after all, to solve them.

ITIL exams

In 2007 the APM Group launched a new certification scheme for ITIL, based on ITIL version 3. ITIL version 2 will be maintained for a transition period, continuing until the year 2008. **ITIL version 2** has qualifications on three levels:
* **Foundation** Certificate in IT Service Management
* **Practitioner** Certificate in IT Service Management
* **Manager** Certificate in IT Service Management

Until 2000, some 60,000 ITIL certificates had been distributed and by 2006 the number had reached 500,000 certificates .

For **ITIL version 3** a new system of qualifications has been set up. There are four qualification levels:
* Foundation Level
* Intermediate Level (Lifecycle Stream & Capability Stream)
* ITIL Diploma
* Advanced Service Management Professional Diploma

For more information about the ITIL V3 Qualification Scheme, see http://www.itil-officialsite.com/Qualifications/ITILV3QualificationScheme.asp.

2.2 IT governance

With the growing role of information, information systems and IT service management, the management requirements for IT grew as well. These requirements focus on two aspects: the compliance with internal and external policies, laws and regulations, and the provision of added value to the stakeholders of the organization. IT governance is still a very young discipline, with no more than a few acknowledged standards or frameworks available. In contrast, there are many different definitions of IT governance available. A definition that receives a lot of support is the one by Van Grembergen:

> **IT governance** consists of a comprehensive framework of structures, processes and relational mechanisms. Structures involve the existence of responsible functions such as IT executives and accounts, and a diversity of IT Committees. Processes refer to strategic IT decision-making and monitoring. Relational mechanisms include business/IT participation and partnerships, strategic dialogue and shared learning.

There is a clear distinction between governance and management, suggesting that governance enables the creation of a setting in which others can manage their tasks effectively (Sohal & Fitzpatrick). So IT governance and IT management are two separate entities. IT service management can be considered to be part of the IT management domain, which leaves IT governance in the business or information management domain.

Although many frameworks are characterized as "IT Governance frameworks", such as COBIT and even ITIL, most of them are in fact management frameworks. There is at least one standard for IT Governance available: the local Australian standard for Corporate governance of information and communication technology (AS8015-2005).

2.3 Organizational maturity

From the moment **Richard Nolan** introduced his "staged model" for the application of IT in organizations in 1973, many people have used stepwise improvement models. These models were quickly recognized as suitable instruments for quality improvement programs, thereby helping organizations to climb up the maturity ladder.

Dozens of variations on the theme can easily be found, ranging from trades such as software development, acquisition, systems engineering, software testing, website development, data warehousing and security engineering, to help desks and knowledge management. Obviously the *kaizen* principle (improvement works best in smaller steps) was one that appealed to many.

After Nolan's staged model in 1973, the most appealing application of this modeling was found when the Software Engineering Institute (SEI) of Carnegie Mellon University, USA, published its Software Capability Maturity Model (SW-CMM). The CMM was copied and applied in most of the cases mentioned above, making CMM something of a standard in maturity modeling. The CMM was later followed by newer editions, including CMMI (CMM Integration).

Later, these models were applied in quality management models, like the European Foundation for Quality Management (EFQM). Apart from the broad quality management models, there are several other industry accepted practices, such as Six Sigma and Total Quality Management (TQM) which are complementary to ITIL.

The available standards, and frameworks of best practice, offer guidance for organizations in achieving "operational excellence" in IT service management. Depending upon their stage of development, organizations tend to require different kinds of guidance.

Maturity model: CMMI

In the IT industry, the process maturity improvement process is best known in the context of the **Capability Maturity Model Integration** (**CMMI**). This process improvement method was developed by the Software Engineering Institute (SEI) of Carnegie Mellon University. CMMI provides both a staged and a continuous model. In the continuous representation, improvement is measured using capability levels. Maturity is measured for a particular process across an organization. In the staged representation, improvement is measured using maturity levels, for a set of processes across an organization.

The capability levels in the **CMMI continuous representation** are:
- **incomplete process** - a process that either is not performed or partially performed
- **performed process** - satisfies the specific goals of the process area
- **managed process** - a performed (capability level 1) process that has the basic infrastructure in place to support the process
- **defined process** - a managed (capability level 2) process that is tailored from the organization's set of standard processes according to the organization's tailoring guidelines, and contributes work products, measures and other process improvement information to the organizational process assets
- **quantitatively Managed process** - a defined (capability level 3) process that is controlled using statistical and other quantitative techniques
- **optimizing process** - a quantitatively managed (capability level 4) process that is improved based on an understanding of the common causes of variation inherent in the process

The **CMMI staged representation** model defines five maturity levels, each a layer in the base for the next phase in the ongoing process improvement, designated by the numbers 1 through 5:
- **initial** - processes are ad hoc and chaotic
- **managed** - the projects of the organization have ensured that processes are planned and executed in accordance with policy
- **defined** - processes are well characterized and understood, and are described in standards, procedures, tools and methods

- **quantitatively managed** - the organization and projects establish quantitative objectives for quality and process performance, and use them as criteria in managing processes
- **optimizing** - focuses on continually improving process performance through incremental and innovative process and technological improvements

Many other maturity models were based on these structures, such as the Gartner Maturity Models. Most of these models are focused at capability maturity. Some others, like KPMG's World Class IT Maturity Model, take a different approach.

Standard: ISO/IEC 20000

Developing and maintaining a quality system which complies with the requirements of the ISO 9000 (ISO-9000:2000) series can be considered a tool for the organization to reach and maintain the system-focused (or "managed" in IT Service CMM) level of maturity. These ISO standards emphasize the definition, description and design of processes. For IT service management organizations, a specific ISO standard was produced: the ISO/ IEC 20000 (see Figure 2.1).

Figure 2.1 Overview of the ISO/IEC 20000 service management system

Customer maturity

When assessing the maturity of an organization, we cannot restrict ourselves to the service provider. The **level of maturity of the customer** (Figure 2.2) is also important. If there are large differences in maturity between the provider and the customer, then these will have to be considered to prevent a mismatch in the approach, methods and mutual expectations. Specifically, this affects the communication between the customer and the provider.

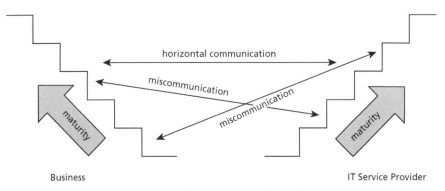

Figure 2.2 Communication and maturity levels: customer and provider

2.4   Benefits and risks of ITSM frameworks

The list below identifies some benefits and possible problems of using IT service management best practices. This list is not intended to be definitive, but is provided here as a basis for considering some of the benefits that can be achieved and some of the mistakes that can be made when using common process-based IT service management frameworks:

Benefits to the customer/user:
- The provision of IT services becomes more customer-focused and agreements about service quality improve the relationship.
- The services are described better, in customer language, and in more appropriate detail.
- Better management of the quality, availability, reliability and cost of the services are managed better.
- Communication with the IT organization is improved by agreeing on the points of contact.

Benefits to the IT organization:
- The IT organization develops a clearer structure, becomes more efficient, and is more focused on the corporate objectives.
- The IT organization is more in control of the infrastructure and services it has responsibility for, and changes become easier to manage.
- An effective process structure provides a framework for the effective outsourcing of elements of the IT services.
- Following best practices encourages a cultural change towards providing service, and supports the introduction of quality management systems based on the ISO 9000 series or on ISO/IEC 20000.
- Frameworks can provide coherent frames of reference for internal communication and communication with suppliers, and for the standardization and identification of procedures.

Potential problems/mistakes:
- The introduction can take a long time and require significant effort, and may require a change of culture in the organization; an overambitious introduction can lead to frustration because the objectives are never met.
- If process structures become an objective in themselves, the service quality may be adversely affected; in this scenario, unnecessary or over-engineered procedures are seen as bureaucratic obstacles, which are to be avoided where possible.
- There is no improvement in IT services due a fundamental lack of understanding about what the relevant processes should provide, what the appropriate performance indicators are, and how processes can be controlled.
- Improvement in the provision of services and cost reductions are insufficiently visible, because no baseline data was available for comparison and/or the wrong targets were identified.
- A successful implementation requires the involvement and commitment of personnel at all levels in the organization; leaving the development of the process structures to a specialist department may isolate that department in the organization and it may set a direction that is not accepted by other departments.
- If there is insufficient investment in appropriate training and support tools, justice will not be done to the processes and the service will not be improved; additional resources and personnel may be needed in the short term if the organization is already overloaded by routine IT service management activities which may not be using "best practices".

2.5   Service Lifecycle: concept and overview

The information provision role and system has grown and changed since the launch of ITIL version 2 (in 2000/02). IT supports and is part of an increasing number of goods and services. In the business world, the information provision role has changed as well: IT's role is no longer just supporting, but has become the baseline for the creation of business value.

ITIL version 3 intends to include and provide insight into IT's new role in all its complexity and dynamics. To that end, a new service management approach has been chosen that does not center around processes, but focuses on the Service Lifecycle.

Basic concepts

Before we describe the Service Lifecycle, we need to define some basic concepts.

Good practice

ITIL is presented as a good practice (literally: correct method). This is an approach or method that has proven itself in practice. These good practices can be a solid backing for organizations that want to improve their IT services. In such cases, the best thing to do is to select a generic standard or method that is accessible to everyone, ITIL, COBIT, CMMI, PRINCE2® and ISO/IEC 20000, for example. One of the benefits of these freely accessible generic standards is that they can be applied to several real-life environments and situations. There is also ample training available for open standards. This makes it much easier to train staff.

Another source for good practice is proprietary knowledge. A disadvantage of this kind of knowledge is that it may be customized for the context and needs of a specific organization. Therefore, it may be difficult to adopt or replicate and it may not be as effective in use.

Service

A service is about creating value for the customer. ITIL defines a service as follows:

> *A **service** is a means of delivering value to customers by facilitating outcomes the customers want to achieve without the ownership of specific costs or risks.*

Outcomes are possible from the performance of tasks, and they are limited by a number of constraints. Services enhance performance and reduce the pressure of constraints. This increases the chances of the desired outcomes being realized.

Value

Value is the core of the service concept. From the customer's perspective value consists of two core components: utility and warranty. Utility is what the customer receives, and warranty is how it is provided. The concepts utility and warranty are described in the Section "Service Strategy".

Service management

ITIL defines service management as follows:

> **Service management** is a set of specialized organizational capabilities for providing value to customers in the form of services.

ITIL discusses some of the fundamental principles of service management that supplement the functions and processes in the ITIL core books. The next principles may help design a service management system:

- **Specialization & coordination** - The goal of service management is to make capabilities and resources available through services that are useful and acceptable to the customer with regard to quality, costs and risks. The service provider takes the weight of responsibility and resource management off the customer's shoulders so that they can focus on the business' core competence. Service management coordinates the business of service management responsibility with regard to certain resources. *Utility* and *warranty* act as a guide.

- **Agency principle** - Service management always involves an agent and a principal that seconds this agent to fulfill activities on their behalf. Agents may be consultants, advisors or service providers. Service agents act as intermediary between service providers and customers in conjunction with users. Usually, these agents are the service provider's staff, but they can also be self-service systems and processes for users. Value for the customer is created through agreements between principals and agents.

- **Encapsulation** - The customer's interest focuses on the value of use; he prefers to be spared from any technical details and structure complexity. The "encapsulation principle" is focused on hiding what the customer does not need and showing what is valuable and useful to the customer. Three principles are closely linked to this:
  - separation of concerns
  - modularity: a clear, modular structure
  - loose coupling: reciprocal independence of resources and users

Systems

ITIL describes the organizational structure concepts which proceed from system theory. The Service Lifecycle in ITIL version 3 is a system; however, a function, a process or an organization is a system as well. The definition of a system:

> A **system** is a group of interacting, interrelating, or interdependent components that form a unified whole, operating together for a common purpose.

Feedback and learning are two key aspects in the performance of systems; they turn processes, functions and organizations into dynamic systems. Feedback can lead to learning and growth, not only within a process, but also within an organization in its entirety.

Within a process, for instance, the feedback about the performance of one cycle is, in its turn, input for the next process cycle. Within organizations, there can be feedback between processes, functions and lifecycle phases. Behind this feedback is the common goal: the customer's objectives.

Functions and processes

The distinction between functions and processes is important in ITIL.

What is a function?

> A **function** is a subdivision of an organization that is specialized in fulfilling a specified type of work, and is responsible for specific end results.
> Functions are independent subdivisions with capabilities and resources that are required for their performance and results. They have their own practices and their own knowledge body.

What is a process?

> A **process** is a structured set of activities designed to accomplish a defined objective.
> Processes result in a goal-oriented change, and utilize feedback for self-enhancing and self-corrective actions.

Processes possess the following characteristics:
- They are **measurable** because they are performance-oriented.
- They have **specific results**.
- They provide results to **customers** or stakeholders.
- They **respond to a specific event** - a process is indeed continual and iterative, but is always originating from a certain event.

It can be difficult to determine whether something is a function or a process. According to ITIL, whether it is a function or process depends completely on the organizational design. A good example of a function is a service desk, a good example of a process is change management.

The hierarchical structure of functions can lead to the rise of "silos" in which each function is very self-oriented. This does not benefit the success of the organization as a whole. Processes run through the hierarchical structure of functions; functions often share some processes. This is how processes suppress the rise of functional silos, and help to ensure an improved coordination in between functions.

The Service Lifecycle

ITIL version 3 approaches service management from the lifecycle of a service. The Service Lifecycle is an organization model providing insight into:
- the way service management is structured
- the way the various lifecycle components are linked to each other
- the impact that changes in one component will have on other components and on the entire lifecycle system

So the new ITIL version focuses on the Service Lifecycle, and the way service management components are linked. The processes are also discussed (both the old familiar ones and the new ones) in the cycle phases. They describe how things change.

The Service Lifecycle consists of five phases. Each volume of the new ITIL books describes one of these phases:

1. **Service Strategy** - the phase of designing, developing and implementing service management as a strategic resource
2. **Service Design** - the design phase of developing appropriate IT services, including architecture, processes, policy and documents; the design goal is to meet the current and future business requirements
3. **Service Transition** - the phase of developing and improving capabilities for the transition of new and modified services to production

4. **Service Operation** - the phase of achieving effectiveness and efficiency in providing and supporting services in order to ensure value for the customer and the service provider
5. **Continual Service Improvement** - the phase of creating and maintaining the value for the customer by design improvement, and service introduction and operation

Service Strategy is the axis of the Service Lifecycle (Figure 2.3) that "runs" all other phases; it is the phase of policymaking and objectives. The phases Service Design, Service Transition and Service Operation implement this strategy, their continual theme is adjustment and change. The Continual Service Improvement phase stands for learning and improving, and embraces all cycle phases. This phase initiates improvement programs and projects, and prioritizes them based on the strategic objectives of the organization.

Figure 2.3 The Service Lifecycle

The Service Lifecycle is a combination of many perspectives on the reality of organizations. This offers more flexibility and control.

The dominant pattern in the Service Lifecycle is the succession of Service Strategy to Service Design, to Service Transition and to Service Operation, and then, through Continual Service Improvement, back to Service Strategy, and so on. The cycle encompasses, however, many patterns. Depending on tasks and responsibilities, a manager can choose his own control perspective. If you are responsible for the design, development or improvement of processes, the best perspective to use is a process perspective. If you are responsible for managing SLAs, contracts and services, the Service Lifecycle perspective and its various phases is likely to meet your needs better.

ITIL Library

The official, new style ITIL Library encompasses the following components:

- Core Library - the five Service Lifecycle publications:
  - Service Strategy
  - Service Design
  - Service Transition
  - Service Operation
  - Continual Service Improvement

Each book covers a phase from the Service Lifecycle and encompasses various processes. The processes are always described in detail in the book in which they find their key application.

- Complementary portfolio:
  - introduction guide
  - key element guides
  - qualification aids
  - white papers
  - glossary

CHAPTER 3

Lifecycle Phase: Service Strategy

3.1 Introduction

In this section, the axis of the lifecycle is introduced. Service Strategy delivers guidance with designing, developing and implementing service management as a strategic resource. The Service Strategy is critical in the context of the processes along the ITIL Service Lifecycle in the Service Design, Service Transition, Service Operation, and Continual Service Improvement (CSI) phases.

The Service Strategy gives a more extensive scope of the ITIL framework. Organizations that are already using ITIL can use this section as a guideline for developing a strategic overview of their ITIL-based capabilities. They can also try to improve the synchronization between IT and business strategies. First consider why something should be done before thinking about how it will be done. The why is more important for the client's business.

This section offers a number of guidelines that will help in setting customer- and market-oriented goals and expectations. A Service Strategy also helps in identifying, selecting and prioritizing opportunities. A clear Service Strategy helps to ensure that an organization is equipped to manage costs and risks within the service portfolios.

The following topics are covered: defining the strategy concept; service assets; service catalogues; implementation of the strategy through the Service Lifecycle; various types of service providers; financial management; service portfolio management; organizational development; and strategic risks.

What is strategy?

Strategy is a term that originated in the military world, where it is primarily defined as the distribution and application of military resources in order to meet the objectives of a plan. In service management the strategy also has to maintain the link between policies and tactics.

The goal of Service Strategy is to identify the competition and to compete with them by distinguishing oneself from the rest and by delivering superior performances. ITIL cites the following building blocks of well-performing service providers:

- **market focus** - know where and how to compete
- **distinctive capabilities** - create distinctive and profitable assets that the business appreciates
- **performance anatomy** - organizational standpoints that are measurable and feasible, such as viewing services as a strategic asset in which constant improvement is necessary

The four Ps of strategy

If a service provider really knows its service objectives and understands the distinguishing factors of its product, then it is ready to begin the Service Lifecycle. The Service Strategy constitutes the axis of the cycle. We can begin with what we call the four Ps (based on Mintzberg, 1994); strategy is perspective, position, plan and pattern:

- **perspective** - have a clear vision and focus
- **position** - take a clearly defined stance
- **plan** - form a precise notion of how the organization should develop itself
- **pattern** - maintain consistency in decisions and actions

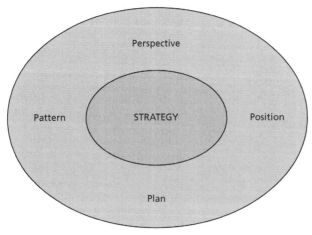

Figure 3.1 The four Ps of strategy, based on Henry Mintzberg

Perspective

Strategy is *perspective* because it provides the vision and focus of an organization. It determines the distinguishing characteristics of the service provider and its interactions with the customer.

> Strategy as **perspective** defines the convictions, values and goals that govern the behavior of the entire organization. A strategic perspective determines the direction through which the service provider can achieve its objectives.

Pose the following questions as a way of testing the perspectives:
- Are they clear and memorable?
- Are they suitable for promoting and conducting activities?
- Do they establish the boundaries within which people are free to experiment?

Position

Strategy is *position* because it provides the decisions that ensure that the services will be offered in a specific market. It is essential that a service provider be conscious of its position in the marketplace.

> Strategy as **position** defines the distinguishing characteristics of the service provider in the eyes of the customer.

Several positions are possible:
- positioning based on **variety** - a limited catalogue of services, but with such depth that diverse customers with similar needs can be adequately served
- positioning based on **needs** - a broad catalogue of services that delivers most of the services to a specific type of customer
- positioning based on **access** - ability to deliver services to customers with specific needs, such as location, scale or structures

Pose the following questions to test the organization's position:
- Does the organization help managers test the suitability of a specific procedure?
- Does the organization set clear boundaries within which personnel may or may not operate?
- Is there a degree of freedom for experimenting within these constraints?

Plan

Strategy is a *plan* because it prescribes how an organization handles a development.

> *Strategy as **plan** focuses on the organization's action plan in a competitive market. Service management is a coordinated set of plans through which service providers plan and implement service strategies.*

Pattern

> *Strategy as **pattern** represents an organization's procedures. As a consequence of the perspective, position, and plan of the strategy, characteristic patterns are created that lead to recurring successes.*

Strategy is a *pattern* because it lays out the activities within the allotted timeframe.

Mission and objectives

Specialization and coordination are necessary in the lifecycle approach. Feedback and monitoring during the various processes of the cycle makes this possible.

The dominant pattern in the cycle is the succession of Service Strategy to Service Design, to Service Transition, to Service Operation and back again to Service Strategy via CSI.

Service Strategy assists organizations to think and do business in a strategic manner. The implementation of the strategy takes place through the use of strategic assets.

Finally, a multidisciplinary approach is necessary in order to answer questions such as:

- What kind of services must we offer, and to whom?
- How do we stand out above the competition?
- How can we justify strategic investments?
- How can we actually create value for the customer and our stakeholders?
- How can we efficiently allocate resources in a service portfolio?
- How can we use financial management to ensure insight and control over value creation?

To survive, organizations must understand how they create value for themselves and for the customer. The mission of the Service Strategy phase is to develop the capacity to achieve and maintain a strategic advantage. The associated objectives are:
- defining strategic objectives
- determining the direction for growth opportunities
- setting investment priorities
- defining outcomes, learning about effectiveness
- creating strategic assets
- identifying the competition
- surpassing the competition by delivering distinctive performances
- devising plans that will ensure dominance over the competition now and in the future

The development and application of the Service Strategy requires constant revision, just as in all other components of the cycle. If the strategy is effective, then the efforts that are expended in all of the other phases of the lifecycle will be successful.

3.2   Basic concepts

Utility and warranty

Value is not only discernable in the customer's business outcomes, but is also, to a large extent, dependent on the customer's perception. This refers to the difference between economic value and economic perception. Perception depends on the customer's self-image, the value attributes, and personal experience. It is important to remember that the definition and differentiation of value are mainly in the mind of the customer. Economic value does not have to correspond automatically with the economic perceptions of the customer.

ITIL version 3 uses two important concepts for the value of a service. For customers, the positive effect is the "utility" of a service; the insurance of this positive effect is the "warranty". The **service value** is a combination of utility and warranty, defined by ITIL as:
- **Utility** - *fitness for purpose*. The attributes of the service that have a positive effect on the performance of activities, objects, and tasks with a specific result. Utility stands for the increase of a possible profit.
- **Warranty** - *fitness for use*. Availability and reliability in continuity and security. Warranty stands for the decline in possible losses.

The utility is what the customer receives, and the warranty affirms how it will be delivered. It is advisable to view these two aspects separately in order to arrive at the best possible design and development. See Figure 3.2 for the combined steps towards value creation.

Figure 3.2 Combining utility and warranty for value creation

Communicating utility and warranty

The utility of a service is communicated through the support of certain results or by preventing certain risks and costs. Customers are very eager to outsource the management of assets that remove financial resources in their core assets. They also want to prevent a shortage in capacity.

Customers are unable to use services that are not suitable for use. Warranty guarantees the utility of a service by ensuring that it is available and that it offers sufficient capacity, continuity and security:

- **Availability** - Availability is the most fundamental aspect in the delivery of services to a customer. It offers the customer the assurance that the services are available according to the agreed terms and conditions.
- **Capacity** - Without the effective monitoring of capacity issues, service providers are not in a position to offer the utility of most services.
- **Continuity** - Continuity ensures that the service supports the business even during times of great difficulty or other disasters.
- **Security** - Security assures the customers that they can make use of the service safely and securely.

Value creation is a combination of the effects of utility and warranty. Both are necessary for the creation of value for the customer. See Figure 3.3 for the effect that the combination of utility and warranty has on the customer's assets.

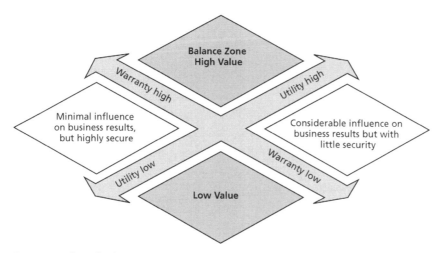

Figure 3.3 Effect of utility and warranty on customer assets

Service structures

The value creation process is complex to such an extent that traditional service models are inadequate. Rather than concentrating on a fixed chronology of activities in a chain, the focus during the Service Strategy phase must be placed on the value creation system itself. Service management stands for patterns of cooperation.

ITIL defines the value network as follows:

> A **value network** is a web of relationships that generates tangible and intangible value through complex and dynamic exchanges through two or more organizations.

The following questions play a role in the construction of a service model:
- Who are the participants in the service?
- What are the patterns in exchanges and transactions?
- What is the impact or what are the products to be delivered from each transaction and each participant?
- What is the best way to generate value?

Service assets

Resources and capabilities

Resources and capabilities are types of assets. Organizations use them to create value in the form of goods and services. Resources comprise the direct input for production. Management, organization, people and knowledge convert resources into value. Capabilities represent the capacity of an organization to coordinate, manage and apply resources in order to produce value.

Resources are often based on experiences; they are knowledge-intensive, based on information, and deeply imbedded in the people, systems, processes and technologies of an organization. It is relatively easy to acquire resources compared to capabilities.

Capabilities develop over the years. The development of distinctive capabilities is stimulated by broadening and deepening of experiences acquired through the number and variety of customer, markets, contracts and services. Experience is gained through problem-solving, handling situations, managing risks and analyzing mistakes. Service providers must develop distinctive capabilities in order to retain customers with services that are difficult to duplicate by the competition. Service providers must also invest substantially in education and training if they are to continue to develop their strategic assets.

Capabilities alone cannot produce value without adequate and appropriate resources. The productive capacity of a service provider depends on the availability of resources. Capabilities are used to develop, implement and coordinate the productive capacity.

Asset types

Together resources and capabilities form the basis for the value of a service (see Figure 3.4).

Below is a list of descriptions of asset types:
- **Management** - Management is a system that includes leadership, administration, policy, performance, regulations and incentives; this layer cultivates, coordinates and oversees other asset types.
- **Organization** - Organizational assets are active configurations of people, processes, applications and infrastructures that implement all organizational activities; this layer includes the functional hierarchies, social networks of groups, teams and individuals, and all of the systems that they use for working together towards collective goals.

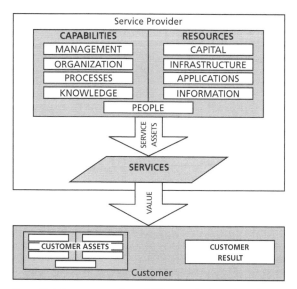

Figure 3.4 Resources and capabilities are the basis for value creation

- **Process** - Process assets consist of algorithms, methods, procedures and routines that drive the implementation and management of activities and interactions.
- **Knowledge** - Knowledge assets are accumulations of realization, experience, information, insight and intellectual property that are associated with specific activities and contexts.
- **People** - People as assets represent the capacity for creativity, analysis, perception, education, assessment, leadership, communication, coordination, empathy and trust.
- **Information** - Information assets are collections, patterns and meaningful abstractions of data that are applied in the context of customers, contracts, services, events, projects and production.
- **Applications** - Application assets are greatly varied in type and include artefacts, automation and tools for supporting the performance of other asset types; applications derive their value from their relationships with other assets.
- **Infrastructure** - Infrastructure assets exist in the form of layers that are defined by their relationships with other assets that they support (people and applications, in particular).
- **Financial capital** - Financial assets are necessary in order to support the ownership or use of all types of assets.

Type of service provider

ITIL distinguishes between the various types of service providers. Although most aspects of service management apply to all types, there are also aspects, such as customers, contracts, competition, markets and incomes, which are different for each type.

ITIL defines the following three archetypes:
- **type I** - internal service provider
- **type II** - Shared Services Unit
- **type III** - external service provider

Type I - Internal service provider

> *Type I providers* *are providers who deliver their services within their own business units.*

Type I providers (Figure 3.5) are found in organizations where IT, R&D, marketing or manufacturing determine the competitive position of the organization, for which a high degree of control is necessary.

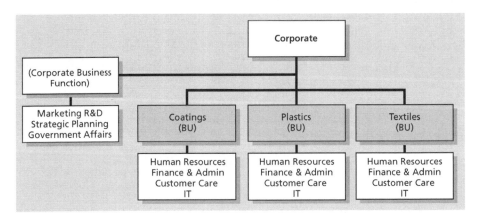

Figure 3.5 Type I providers

Advantages of this type:
- **short lines of communication** - close contact with the customer through which certain costs and risks can be avoided

- **customer-oriented** - specialized in a limited set of business needs, which makes it possible to be very customer-oriented
- **limited decision rights** - decision rights by the manager of the business unit

Disadvantages:
- **limited opportunities for growth** - growth is tied to the growth of the business unit

Competition:
- **open market** - providers outside the business unit

Objective:
- **value contribution** - the attainment of functional excellence and return for the business unit to which they belong

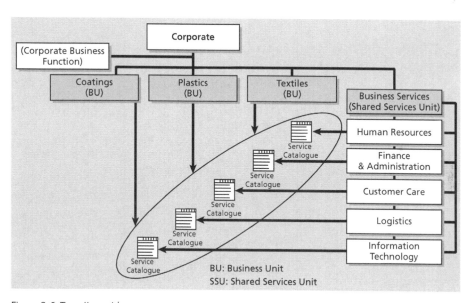

Figure 3.6 Type II provider

Type II - Shared Services Unit (SSU)
Functions such as finance, IT, human resources and logistics are not always at the core of an organization's competitive advantage, and need not be maintained at the corporate level. The services of such shared functions are often consolidated into an autonomous unit called a shared services unit.

> *Type II providers* deliver services to Business Units that operate under the same collective strategy.

The advantages of a Shared Service Unit are (See Figure 3.6):
- **lower prices** - compared with external service providers, through collective benefits, internal agreements and internal bookkeeping
- **broader decision-making authority** - decisions can be made outside the business unit
- **possibility for standardization** - the possibility of the development of a standard, which could be used by various business units
- **competitive position** - possibility of challenging the competition

Disadvantages:
- **replaceable** - customers can compare the provider with external service providers

Objective:
- keep up with the industry's best practice, cultivate the market, formulate business strategies, strive for operational effectiveness and develop distinctive capabilities

Type III - External service provider

> *Type III providers* deliver services to customers in competing business environments that need flexible structures.

Customers come from various places. Competing customers have access to the same assets with the Type III service provider (see Figure 3.7).

Advantages of this type:
- **more flexibility** - more freedom to exploit more opportunities
- **competitive prices** - more opportunities to vary prices
- **minimizing of system risks** - spreading risks over a larger network

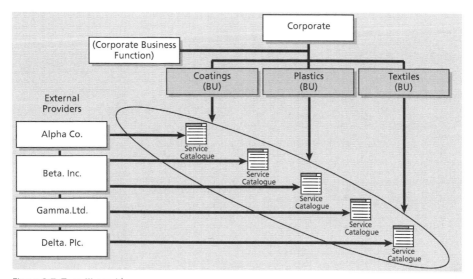

Figure 3.7 Type III provider

Disadvantages:
- greater risks for the customers
- extra costs

Objective:
- to offer customers flexibility and external knowledge, experience, scale, scope, capabilities and resources

Customers consider the following issues when choosing or changing a certain type of service provider (see Figure 3.8):
- Transaction costs:
  - the total costs of a service provider
  - should we keep the activities in-house (aggregation)?
  - should we outsource (disaggregation)?
- strategic factors
- core competencies
- risk management capabilities

From/To	Type I	Type II	Type III
Type I	Functional reorganization	Disaggregation	Outsourcing
Type II	Aggregation	Corporate reorganization	Outsourcing
Type III	Insourcing	Insourcing	Value net reconfiguration

Figure 3.8 Customer's choice of type of service provider

3.3 Processes and other activities

Activities

The following sections deal with the four most important activities of Service Strategy as defined by ITIL (see Figure 3.9):

1. defining the market
   a. understanding the customer
   b. understanding the opportunities
   c. classifying and visualizing the services
2. the development of the offer
3. the development of strategic assets
4. preparation for implementation

Defining the market

In the context of service management, organizations are interested in strategy from two different but connected perspectives. There are strategies for services and there are services for strategies. From the one perspective, strategies are developed for the services that will be offered. From the other perspective, service management is set forth as a competency for a specific business strategy.

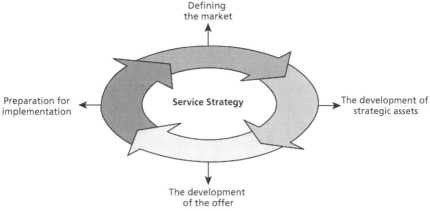

Figure 3.9 The activities of the Service Strategy

Understanding the customer
For service management professionals it is essential to know the performance of the customer's assets. Without an insight into these assets there is no basis on which to determine the value of a service.

Understanding the opportunities
Customers' unsupported objectives can present an opportunity in which services can be developed that could be offered as a solution to the customer's problem.

In a changing business there are new opportunities. The CMS (Configuration Management System) can make the mapping of customer results into services and service assets a viable option.

Having an insight into the customer's business and being familiar with their objectives are essential factors in the development of a strong business relationship with the customer. Business Relation Managers (BRM) are responsible for this. They are closely involved with the customer and manage the opportunities through the use of a Customer Portfolio. BRMs work closely with Product Managers who are responsible for the development and management of services through the lifecycle. Product Managers focus on the products and maintain contact with the business via a service portfolio.

Classifying and visualizing services
Services vary primarily in how and in what context they create value. Service archetypes serve as the business models for services. They define how service providers behave on

behalf of their customers. Customer assets are the context in which value is created because they are the link with the business outcomes that the customer wants.

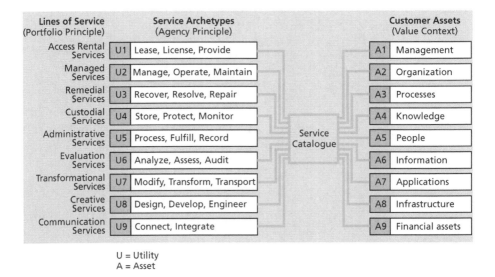

Lines of Service (Portfolio Principle)	Service Archetypes (Agency Principle)		Customer Assets (Value Context)	
Access Rental Services	U1	Lease, License, Provide	A1	Management
Managed Services	U2	Manage, Operate, Maintain	A2	Organization
Remedial Services	U3	Recover, Resolve, Repair	A3	Processes
Custodial Services	U4	Store, Protect, Monitor	A4	Knowledge
Administrative Services	U5	Process, Fulfill, Record	A5	People
Evaluation Services	U6	Analyze, Assess, Audit	A6	Information
Transformational Services	U7	Modify, Transform, Transport	A7	Applications
Creative Services	U8	Design, Develop, Engineer	A8	Infrastructure
Communication Services	U9	Connect, Integrate	A9	Financial assets

U = Utility
A = Asset

Figure 3.10 Service provider business model and customer assets

Depending on a variety of factors, the customer owns various kinds of assets. A combination of a service archetype and a customer asset (see Ux-Ay in Figure 3.10, and Figure 3.11) represents an item in the service catalogue. Various services can be associated with the same archetype.

The same archetype can be used to service a variety of customer assets under a utility-based Service Strategy. This is a variation of needs-based and access-based positioning. The strategy of the service provider determines the contents of the service catalogue.

Service Strategy results in a specific collection of patterns (intended strategy) or a collection of patterns can make a specific Service Strategy attractive (emergent strategy). This visual method is useful in the communication and coordination between the functions and processes of service management. The right synchronization between the value-creating context (customer assets) and the value-creating concepts (service archetype) helps prevent inadequacies in performance.

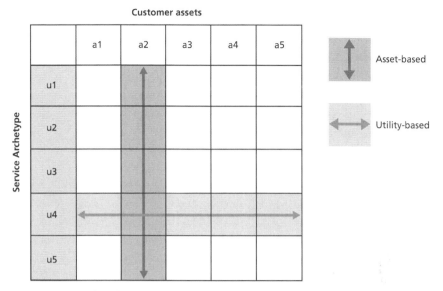

Figure 3.11 Asset-based and utility-based positioning

Developing the offer

The consumers' market

The opportunity for supporting business outcomes with services defines the market. Every market represents a series of opportunities for service providers to serve a customer with one or more services.

Results-oriented definition of services

A results-oriented definition of services ensures that managers view all aspects of service management from the customer's perspective. Services are a way of providing value to customers by facilitating customers' results without having to incur costs and take risks themselves. Well formulated service definitions lead to effective and efficient service management processes.

To ensure that your service definitions are sound, pose the following questions:
- What kind of services do we deliver? (service type)
- Who are our customers? (service type)
- What kinds of results do we support? (utility)
- How do the results create value for the customers of our customers? (utility)
- What constraints do our customers encounter? (utility)

It is impossible to produce value without a complete definition of value.

Service portfolio, pipeline, and catalogue

The service portfolio represents the agreements and investments that the service provider makes with all customers and markets: contractual obligations, service development, Continual Service Improvement (CSI) and third line services (visible or invisible to customers).

The service portfolio also represents all of the resources that are active in the various phases of the Service Lifecycle. An important governance aspect of service portfolio Management (SPM) is that every phase needs resources in order to conclude projects, initiatives and contracts. See the Section on "Processes" for a brief explanation of SPM, or Chapter 5 for a detailed description of SPM and SPM methods.

Summary:

---

*The **service portfolio** represents the opportunities and readiness of a service provider to serve the customers and the market. The service portfolio can be divided into three subsets of services:*
- the service catalogue
- the service pipeline
- retired services

The following sections explain the individual components of the service portfolio.

Figure 3.12 The service portfolio

The service catalogue is the expression of the operational capacity of the provider within the context of a customer or market outlet.

The **service catalogue** has two aspects: the business service catalogue and the technical service catalogue (see Chapter 5 for more details). The business service catalogue portion is defined as the mapping of critical business processes to the underlying IT services, and keeping the details of the relationships between those components, supporting the customer view of the service catalogue. The technical service catalogue is the aspect of the service portfolio that is not visible to the customer, containing details on the technical composition of services, supporting the service provider's view of the service catalogue.

The service catalogue consists of services that are active in the Service Operation phase and those approved to be offered. The service catalogue divides services into components. It communicates the policy, guidelines and accountability, and includes prices, service level agreements, and conditions for delivery.

The service catalogue describes the part of the portfolio in which costs are recovered or profits are earned. The service catalogue also serves as the visualization tool for SPM decisions. The issue of services and the capacity to perform them satisfactorily is also raised in the catalogue. Customer assets and business outcomes trigger questions about the expectations of utility and warranty. If there are items in the catalogue pertaining to whether these expectations can be met, it will result in a service contract or agreement. Catalogue items are clustered in Lines of Service (LOS) based on commonly recurring patterns of business activities (see Figure 3.13).

The approval of the Service Transition is necessary in adding or deleting services from the catalogue for the following reasons:
- If an item is to be added to the catalogue, it must be available if a customer requests it. Due diligence is necessary for ascertaining the comprehensiveness of and support for a proposed service.
- Items in the service catalogue are mainly in the Service Operation phase, with the related contractual obligations to the customer. An evaluation of all changes to the catalogue will be performed to ascertain that all of the necessary obligations have been satisfied.
- The addition of items to the catalogue requires that capabilities and resources be available in order to satisfy a customer's specific request.

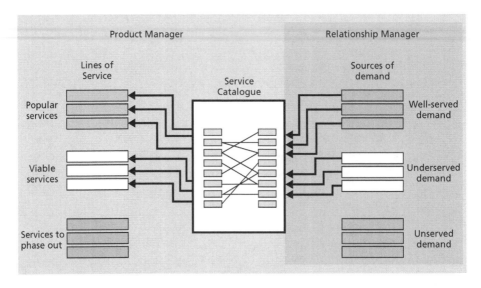

Figure 3.13 Service catalogue, product managers, lines of service, and demand management

The service catalogue is an essential strategy tool because it can be viewed as the virtual projection of the actual and available capabilities of the service provider. Many customers are only interested in what the provider can attest to at this particular moment.

The **service pipeline** consists of services that are still in development for a specific market or customer. These services are to be applied to the operational phase via Service Transition after the finishing of a design-, development-, and test phase. The pipeline represents the growth and strategic anticipation for the future. It says something about the general health of a provider and indicates how new concepts and improvement ideas are nourished through Service Strategy, Service Design, and CSI. Good financial management is necessary in order to finance the pipeline.

Some services in the catalogue are **retired services**, meaning that they have been phased out or withdrawn. The out-phasing of services is a component of Service Transition and occurs in order to guarantee that all agreements with customers will be kept and that the phased out service assets no longer have any contractual obligations.

Developing strategic assets
Service providers must regard service management as a strategic asset. Service management begins with the capabilities that coordinate and manage resources in order

to support a catalogue of services. Capabilities and resources strengthen each other and are modified until the goal of attaining a higher service level is achieved.

Service management as a closed-loop control system
Service management is the capability of an organization to deliver services to customers. Services can improve the performance of customer assets. Improvements in Service Design, Service Transition, and Service Operation enhance the customer performance potential and reduce the risks for the customer.

Services stem from service assets. Service potential is converted into performance potential of customer assets. Enhancing the performance potential often stimulates the request for additional demand for service in terms of scale or scope. This request translates into more use of the service assets and justifies the retention of maintenance activities and upgrades. From this perspective, service management is a closed-loop control system with the following functions:
- developing and maintaining service assets
- understanding the performance potential of customer assets
- mapping of service assets to customer assets through services
- designing, developing and adapting services

Service management as a strategic asset
For service management to be developed as a strategic asset, the value network, within which the service provider operates, must first be identified. This network could exist within only one organization, as is often the case for Type I and Type II providers. More often the value network extends outside the organization's boundaries and includes external customers, providers, and partners.

Strategic assets are dynamic in nature and are expected to continue to perform under changing business conditions and organizational objectives. That makes it necessary for strategic assets to have an instructional capacity. Service management must keep an eye on the interaction between customer assets and service assets (see Figure 3.14).

Increasing the service potential
The service assets of a service provider represent the service potential that is available to customers. One of the core objectives of service management is the improvement of the service potential of the capabilities and resources.

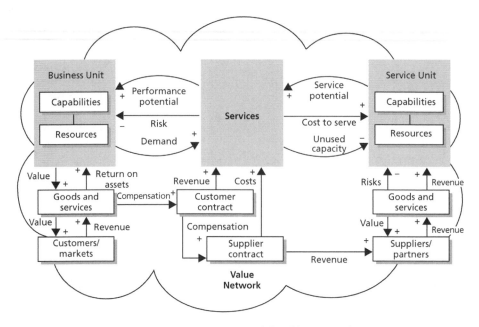

Figure 3.14 Service management as a strategic asset and closed-loop control system

Example: training of personnel increases the service potential as a result of the capability improvement that takes place. This capability improvement is demonstrated in the following aspects:
- The personnel have more knowledge for monitoring and analyzing the lifecycle.
- Resources are improved because personnel are added to the core competencies, and the availability hours of the helpdesk are extended.

Increasing the performance potential

The services of a service provider represent the potential for improving the performance of customer assets. Visualize and define the performance potential of services so that all decisions are focused on the creation of value for the customer.

ITIL poses a number of core questions:
- What is our market?
- What does the market want?
- Do we have something unique to offer to the market?
- Do we have the right portfolio for a specific market?
- Do we have the right catalogue for a specific customer?

- Is every service designed so that it leads to the desired result?
- Is the implementation of every service such that it leads to the desired result?
- Do we have the right models and structures to be a service provider?

Preparation for implementation

Strategic audit

Before formulating a Service Strategy the provider must first look at his distinguishing capabilities:

- Which of our services are the most distinctive?
- Which of our services are the most lucrative?
- Which of our customers and stakeholders are the most satisfied?
- Which of our activities are the most effective?

In this way the strong and weak points can be examined, the Critical Success Factors (CSF) determined, and the risks and opportunities delineated.

Setting goals

Clear objectives ensure consistent decision-making. In order to determine its goals and objectives, an organization must know what the customer wants to achieve. ITIL defines three different types of information that determine the objectives of a service:

- **Tasks** - What is the task of the service that is to be provided?
- **Results** - What kind of results does the customer hope to achieve?
- **Constraints** - What are the limiting factors for the customer in achieving these results?

A clear look at what the customer deems valuable is essential. Look at the service from the outside. Begin with the common business objectives because they lead to a better understanding of the service utility and the service warranty. Customers do not buy services; they buy the satisfaction of a specific need.

Defining the Critical Success Factors (CSFs)

For every market there are critical success factors that determine the success or failure of a Service Strategy. These factors are influenced by customer needs, business trends, competition, regulations, providers, standards, best practices and technologies. ITIL contends that critical success factors, also known as Strategic Industry Factors (SIF), share the following general characteristics:

- They are defined in terms of capabilities and resources
- They seem to be the key to success for market leaders

- They are defined at the market level
- They are the basis for competition among rivals
- They are dynamic
- They usually require considerable investment and development time
- Their value is calculated through a combination with other factors

Critical success factors change or are influenced by one or more of the following factors:
- customers
- competition
- suppliers
- regulators

In every market service providers need a series of core assets in order to support the customer's portfolio with a service portfolio (see Figure 3.15).

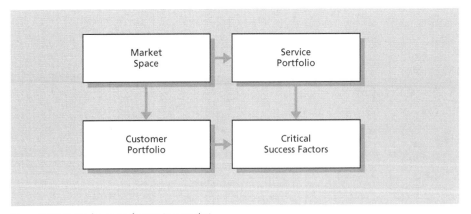

Figure 3.15 Critical success factors in a market

Critical success factors are decisive for success in a market. They are also useful for evaluating the strategic position of a service provider. This means that the critical success factors must be even further defined in specific value propositions to the customer.

Example: to be competitive in a market, it can be necessary to have a high availability; a "fail-safe operation" of the IT infrastructure is essential; and an adequate capacity is needed to guarantee continuity.

In many markets cost effectiveness is a customary Critical Success Factor, while in other markets the specialized domain knowledge or reliability of the infrastructure is much more important.

ITIL advises that a strategic analysis be performed for every market, major customer and service portfolio in order to determine the current strategic positions and the desired strategic positions for success.

Investigation of business potential
Service providers can be active in more than one market. A component of strategic planning is the analysis of the presence in various markets: an analysis of strong and weak points, opportunities and risks in every market. Service providers also analyze the possible expansion of the potential market.

Providers determine which customer needs can be effectively and efficiently satisfied by their services, while at the same time deciding which markets will be served and which will be ignored.
First, identify the:
* markets that can best be served with existing assets
* markets that must be avoided with the existing assets

Next determine for the selected markets:
* what is the service offering (service portfolio)
* which customers (customer portfolio)
* critical success factors
* underserved market spaces
* service models and service assets
* service pipeline and service catalog

Synchronizing with the customer's needs
It is essential to understand the relationship between the customer and market. Customers can cover one or more markets. Markets can include one or more customer.
* The market of type I providers is internal to the organizational unit of which it is a part.
* The market of type II providers is internal to the enterprise, but is distributed through the business units.
* The market of type III providers is divided over more than one enterprise.

Expansion and growth

When service strategies happen to be linked with a market, it is easier to make decisions about portfolios, designs, production and long-term improvement. The growth and expansion of a business is less risky when it is based on core capabilities and proven performance. Successful strategies for expansion are often based on the effective use of service assets and customer portfolios.

Growth in a specific market is made possible through:
- extensions of existing contracts
- increasing requests
- expansion with complementary services

Processes

ITIL version 3 distinguishes three processes at the strategic level:
- Financial management
- Demand management
- Service portfolio management

These processes will be described briefly here; detailed information on them can be found in Chapter 5 of this book.

Financial management

Financial management is an integral component of service management. It anticipates the essential management information that is required for the guarantee of efficient and cost-effective service delivery. Efficient financial management positions the organization to responsibly account for all expenditures and to apply it directly to services.

How can we use financial management to ensure insights into the value creation process? Service valuation ensures that the business understands precisely what is being delivered through IT. Utility and warranty must be translated into a monetary figure in order to calculate the value. ITIL defines two essential value concepts for service valuation: the **provisioning value** (the production costs) and the **service value potential** (the value-adding component).

One objective of financial management is to ensure that the right financing is obtained for the delivery and purchase of services. A plan provides the financial translation and qualification of the anticipated demand for IT services.

ITIL divides planning into three primary areas, each of which represents the financial results that are necessary for continued transparency and service valuation: operating & capital planning, demand planning, and regulatory & environmental. A careful plan leads to confidence that the financial data and models will provide accurate information on the development of demand and the supply of services.

Investment analysis

The objective of the investment analysis (Service Investment) is to derive a value-indication of a specific service from the attained value and incurred costs of the total lifecycle.

Accounting

Financial management builds a bridge between collective financial systems and service management. The results from a service oriented bookkeeping function is that far more details and understanding are obtained in regard to the delivery and consumption of services and the production of data that are directly relevant to the planning process.

Variable Cost Dynamics (VCD)

Variable Cost Dynamics (VCD) focuses on analyzing and understanding the many variables that influence service costs. The VCD analysis can be used as an analysis of the anticipated impact of events such as acquisitions, disinvestments and changes to the service portfolio or service alternative.

Fundamental decisions for financial management

Some of the concepts in financial management have a significant impact on the development of service strategies. ITIL explains a number of these concepts so that every organization can decide which options are best suited to their own service strategies:

- Cost recovery, value center, or accounting center?
- Chargeback: to charge or not to charge.
- Financial management implementation checklist.

For detailed information on financial management, see Chapter 5. One of the greatest challenges in the search for financing for ITIL projects is the identification of a specific business objective that is dependent on service management. For a description of the techniques of return on investment (ROI), post ROI, and business case, see the section on "Methods, techniques and tools" later in this chapter.

Demand Management (DM)

Demand management is an essential aspect of service management in which the offer is harmonized with the demand. The goal of demand management is to predict as accurately as possible the purchase of products, and if possible, to regulate it. Poorly managed demand is a risk for service providers because excess capacity can result in costs that will not be compensated in value. Insufficient capacity, on the other hand, influences the quality of the delivered services and limits the growth of the service. Service Level Agreements (SLAs), demand forecasting, planning and close coordination with the customer can minimize the uncertainty regarding demand, but cannot eliminate it completely.

Service management has an additional problem of synchronous production and consumption. Service Operation is not possible without the existence of the demand for the product to be consumed.

Demand management based on activities

Business processes are the primary source of the demand for services. Patterns of Business Activity (PBA) influence the demand pattern. It is crucial to study the customer's business in order to identify, analyze and record these patterns, which can serve as a solid foundation on which to create a capacity management strategy.

Service packages

Core services deliver the basic results to the customer. They represent the value that the customer wants and for which they are willing to pay. Core services serve as the basis for the value proposition for the customer. Support services make that value proposition possible (enabling service or "basic factors") or improve it (enhancing services or "excitement factors"). The bundling of core services and support services is an essential aspect of a marketing strategy. Service providers must conduct a thorough analysis of the principal conditions in their business environment, the needs of the customer segment or the customer types that they serve, and the alternatives that are available to these customers. These decisions are strategic because they comprise the long-term vision that will enable the continued creation of value for customers in the form of business methods, norms and standards, technologies and regulations in a changing industry. The bundling of support services with core services influences the service-production and provides a challenge for the design-, transition-, and CSI phases.

Service packages come with one or more Service Level Packages (SLP). Each SLP covers a definitive level of utility and warranty from the perspective of the customers' results, assets and the Patterns of Business Activity (PBA). Every SLP is able to provide for one or more demand pattern.

See Chapter 5 for more detailed information on demand management.

Service Portfolio Management (SPM)
SPM is a method to manage all service management investments. The objective of SPM is to achieve maximum value creation while at the same time managing the risks and costs.

SPM begins with the documentation of the standardized services of the organization, and in particular, the service catalogue. To be financially feasible, the portfolio must include the right mix of services in the pipeline and a catalogue.

Business value of SPM
The value of a service portfolio strategy is the capacity to anticipate changes while maintaining the strategy and planning.

SPM is a dynamic and ongoing process and comprises the following work methods:
- **Define** - Inventory the services and business cases, and validate the portfolio data; the cyclical nature of the SPM process means that this phase not only inventories the services, but also continually revalidates the data.
- **Analyze** - Maximize the value of the portfolio; synchronize, and set priorities, and balance from request to offer; in this phase, the strategic objectives take shape.
- **Approve** - Completion of the proposed portfolio, authorization of services and resources; decisions for the future.
- **Charter** - Communication of decisions, allocation of resources, and charter services.

See Chapter 5 for an extended description of the service portfolio management process.

3.4 Organization

IT organizations are complex systems within a greater complex system of the business, customers and industry. The transaction costs principle is a simple but powerful way for organizations to explain that the organization's right to exist is easier to justify if the organization is in a position to manage its transaction costs. An adequate amount of resources, a well-considered strategy, and distinctiveness combine to position the organization to deliver superior services in a competitive market while justifying the acquisition of additional resources. See Figure 3.16 for an illustration of this cycle.

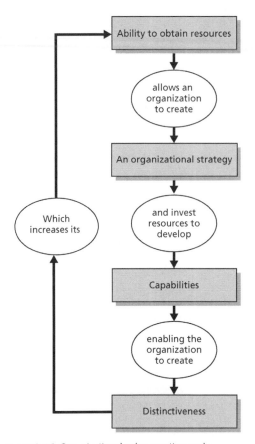

Figure 3.16 Organizational value creation cycle

The development of an organization

There is not just one way for a company to organize itself. External factors have a significant impact on an organization's Service Strategy. A Service Strategy is the implicit blueprint of the design, the size and the scope of an organization.

Organizations characterize themselves by the dominant management style in which the style corresponds with what the organization needs at a specific moment in time.

ITIL describes five recognizable phases in organizational development along the spectrum of centralization and decentralization. It is essential to know the situation in which the organization finds itself and the range of opportunities.

Phase 1: Network

In phase 1, an organization focuses on fast, informal and *ad hoc* provision of services. The organization is technologically oriented and is uncomfortable with formal structures. For organizations in stage 1 innovation and entrepreneurship are important organizational values.

When the demand for service increases, this model is no longer effective. A network structure is a cluster for the coordination of activities through the making of agreements rather than through formal hierarchies or authority. Staff work closely together in order to complement their capabilities.

Advantages of a network structure:
- avoid high bureaucratic costs associated with complex organizations
- a flat organization in which fewer managers are necessary
- flexibility allows for quick modifications or changes to the structure

Disadvantages of a network structure:
- managers must oversee the integration of activities
- significant coordination problems
- opportunities for outsourcing functional activities

Advice: a change in leadership style is necessary to grow beyond these challenges.

Phase 2: Directive

The phase 1 crisis can be resolved with a strong management team. They assume the responsibility for leading the strategy and for guiding managers to embrace their functional responsibilities. Phase 2 focuses on the establishment of hierarchical structures (line management) that differentiate functional activities. Communication is more formal and various basic processes are used.

The turning point arises if an autonomous crisis emerges because centralization hinders decision-making, and there is no longer the freedom for experimentation or innovation.

Advice: to grow beyond this challenge, more delegation is necessary

Phase 3: Delegation

In phase 3, efforts are made to enhance technical efficiency and provide space for innovation in order to reduce costs and improve services. A decentralized organizational structure is adopted in which the responsibility shifts from functional ownership (line management) to process ownership.

A drawback of Phase 3 is that the objectives of functional ownership and process ownership do not coincide. Functional owners have the feeling that they are losing control. For this reason, the process is usually abandoned.

Advice: improve the coordination within the organization by initiating formal systems and programs

Phase 4: Coordination
In phase 4 the focus is directed towards the use of formal systems as a means of achieving better coordination. Centralization of technical functions and decentralization of service management processes emerge, with the goal of improving response time to market demands.

Advice: if everything is in order internally, the next order of business is to improve cooperation with the customer

Phase 5: Collaboration
During Phase 5, the focus is on the improvement of cooperation with the business. A commonly used structure is the matrix structure with the flow of functional responsibilities (line management) on the vertical line, and the flow of product- or customer-related responsibilities on the horizontal line. An organization with a matrix structure takes on all of the functions that it needs.

Advantages of a matrix structure:
• minimizes and overcomes functional barriers
• increases speed of response to changing product- or customer needs
• opens up communication among the functional specialists
• creates opportunities for team members of diverse functions to learn from each other
• uses the skills of specialist staff who can move from product to product and from customer to customer

Disadvantages of a matrix structure:
• lack of a monitoring structure that the staff can use to build a stable pattern of expectations
• conflicting roles can demoralize staff
• possible conflict situation between functions and product- or customer teams

From work group to department

If a work group grows to the size of a department, then the groups can be divided according to attributes. See Table 3.1 for an overview of the basic organizational structures.

Basic structure	Description	Strategic considerations
Function	Organizing by function is the best way of specializing. Pooling of resources and minimizing duplication.	• Specialization • Development of standards • Small-scale
Product	Organizing by product is preferred by organizations that are focused on new and diverse products. This organization is found primarily in processing industries.	• Focus on product • Strong product knowledge
Market or customer	Organizing by market or customer offers differentiation in the form of increased knowledge and response to the wishes of the customer.	• Service is unique for each segment • Customer service • Powerful consumer • Quick service
Geography	Organizing by geography is preferred when providing services in close proximity. Minimizes travel and distribution costs while benefiting from knowledge of local area.	• On-site services • Close to customers for delivery and support • Organization is viewed so a local enterprise
Process	Organizing by process is preferred in executing processes from start of finish.	• Need to shorten process cycle time • Process excellence

Table 3.1 Basic organizational structures

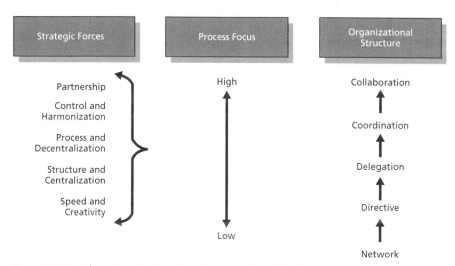

Figure 3.17 Matching strategic strengths with organizational development

Organization design

The key to organizational design is strategy. The strategy determines the focus and leads the criteria for every step in the design process. The first order of business is to determine the departmental structure for designing the core processes (Figure 3.17).

Organizational culture

The culture of an organization is a set of collective values and norms that determine the course of both internal and external interactions. A collective culture contributes to the effectiveness of the organization. There are two types of values:

- **end values** - the desired results in terms of quality, excellence, reliability, innovation, and profitability
- **instrumental values** - the desired behavior in terms of standards, respect for tradition and authority, careful and conservative treatment and moderation

You can analyze the culture of a service management organization as follows:

- determine the end values and the instrumental values
- determine whether the objectives, norms and regulations carry over the values of the organizational culture to the personnel
- assess whether new staff is immediately accepted into the organizational culture

Sourcing strategy

The goal of the Service Strategy is to improve the core competencies. Sometimes it is more efficient to outsource certain services. We call this the SOC principle (separation of concerns, SOC): that which results from the search for competitive differentiation through the redistribution of resources and capabilities.

A risk in outsourcing of services is outsourcing them to a competitor:

- **Substitution** - The vendor can replace the sourcing organization.
- **Disruption** - The vendor can damage your reputation.
- **Distinctiveness** - You can develop a dependence on another organization.

Outsourcing structures

The dynamic of the outsourcing of services requires that organizations formally determine the provisions of an outsourcing strategy. This also includes the structure and role of the relevant party, and the impact of outsourcing on decision-making. The following generic forms of outsourcing can be delineated:

- **internal outsourcing**:
  - Type 1 internal - provision and delivery of services by internal staff; this offers the most control, but is limited in scale

- Type 2 shared services - working with internal BUs; offers lower costs than Type 1 and more standardization, but is still limited in scale
- **traditional outsourcing**:
  - complete outsourcing of a service - a single contract with one service provider; better in terms of scaling opportunities, but limited in best-in-class capabilities
- **multi-vendor outsourcing**:
  - *prime* - a single contract with one service provider who works with multiple providers; improved capabilities and risks, but increased complexity
  - *consortium* - a selection of multiple service providers; the advantage is best-in-class with more oversight; the disadvantage is the risk of the necessity of working with the competition
  - *selective outsourcing* - a pool of service providers selected and managed through the service receiver; this is the most difficult structure to manage
  - *co-sourcing* - a variation of selective outsourcing in which the service receiver combines a structure of internal or shared services with external providers; in this case, the service receiver is the service integrator

In outsourcing services a balance must be found between acceptable risks and control.

Outsourcing with multiple providers
It appears that outsourcing with multiple providers is a good method because the organization can maintain strong relationships with each provider while the risks are spread out and costs are contained. The challenge is the governance and management of these relationships.

Checklist for the selection of providers:
- **demonstrated competencies** - staff, use of technology, innovation, experience, and certification, where applicable
- **track record** - quality, financial value, dedication
- **relationship dynamics** - do the vision and strategy fit with those of the organization?
- **quality of solutions** - have the services been delivered as requested?
- **overall capabilities** - financial stability, resources, management systems, scope and range of services

Service Provider Interfaces (SPI)
Various guidelines and reference points are necessary to support the development of business relationships. Service provider interfaces offer these reference points.

During contract discussions the responsibilities and service levels should be negotiated:
- identification of integration points of various management processes
- identification of specific roles and responsibilities
- identification of management information that is relevant to the customer

Process owners possess SPIs and define and maintain them. SPI definitions consist of:
- technological prerequisites (e.g. management tool standards or prescribed protocols)
- data requirements (e.g. specific events or records), formats (data layout), interfaces (e.g. APIs, firewall ports), and protocols (e.g. SNMP, XML)
- non-negotiable requirements
- required roles/responsibilities
- response times and escalation paths

Sourcing governance
Governance is the framework of decision rights that encourage the desired behavior in outsourcing. The difference between governance and management is that management has to do with decision-making and the implementation of processes; governance has to do with making the right decisions.

Governance is often forgotten and is therefore the weakest link in the service sourcing strategy. With a few simple interventions, the first inroad towards governance can be made:
- **establish a governance body** - decisions can be made on the right level
- **differentiate between governance domains** - with distinctions according to important domains, such as service delivery, communication, and contract management
- **establish a fixed decision rights matrix** - RACI- or RASIC-matrices are the most common forms for decision rights matrices

ISO/IEC 20000 is the first formal international standard specifically designed for IT service management. It provides a foundation for the management structure between internal- and external providers, therefore minimizing the risks with service sourcing. It is especially useful in multisource environments.

Critical success factors
The factors of an outsourcing strategy often depend on:
- desired results
- optimum model for delivering services
- best location from which to deliver services

Recommended approach of the strategy:
- analyze the internal service management competencies of the organization
- compare these findings with the industry benchmarks
- examine the organization's ability to deliver strategic value

To measure the effect of sourcing, the organization must conduct a zero-measure of its performance metrics before commencing implementation. This can be established with two types of metrics:
- **business metrics** - financial savings, service level improvements, business process efficiency
- **customer metrics** - availability and consistency of services, more supply, service quality

Roles and responsibilities
A key role in the implementation of a sourcing strategy lies with the Chief Sourcing Officer, who reports to the CIO and manages the implementation of sourcing. Other important roles may include:
- **Director of service management** - The director supervises the provider on behalf of the business.
- **Contract manager** - The contract manager manages the service contract from the perspective of the service provider.
- **Product manager** - The product manager manages the services in the service provider's organization.
- **Process owner** - The process owner manages the process models that have been developed on behalf of the users
- **Business representatives** - They represent the customers' interests and manage the sourcing relationship from that perspective.

3.5 Methods, techniques and tools
Services are socio-technical systems with service assets as the operational elements. The interactions between two sub-systems in the form of dependencies (passive) and influences (active) are critical for the performance of service management as value-creating systems.

The effectiveness of the Service Strategy depends on a well-managed relationship between the social and technical sub-systems. It is essential to identify and manage these dependencies and influences. Reviews of Service Design, Service Transition, Service Operation, and CSI must include an analysis of possible dysfunction or lack of synchronicity between the two sub-systems. The interest of a balanced approach is apparent from the following observations:

- Improvements in the design and the realization of activities, tasks and interfaces can compensate for inadequacies in human resources.
- Investing in knowledge, skills, behavior and experience can compensate for poorly designed systems.
- Automation of routine activities can reduce unwanted discrepancies and relieve work pressure through a simple technical adjustment.

The design of socio-technical systems is an important consideration in service management. It is important to know that services are much more than a series of activities that produce a certain value. They are systems with complex interactions between different production factors and service assets.

Service automation

Automation can have a significant impact on the performance of service assets such as management, organization, people, processes, knowledge and information.

Service management can benefit from automation in the following areas: design and modeling, service catalogues, identifying and analyzing patterns, classification, investigation and optimization.

To prepare for automation, ITIL recommends the following steps:

- Simplify the service processes before automating, but be careful not to lose any essential information.
- Clarify the flow of activities, allocation of tasks, need for information and interactions.
- In self-service situations, minimize the area in which users come into contact with the underlying systems and processes.
- Do not rush the implementation of automation when it involves tasks and interactions that are not simple and routine.

Service analysis and instrumentation

Service analysis is the placing of information in a context of patterns. Through an understanding of patterns of information we can answer the following questions:

- How does this incident influence the service?
- How does this incident impact the business?
- How should we respond?

In this case, the Data-Information-Knowledge-Wisdom (DIKW) sequence can be used. This series describes the added value that can be given to the data by viewing them in this context.

Instrumentation describes the technologies and techniques that are used to evaluate the behavior of infrastructure elements. Instrumentation can aggregate a very large amount of basic data, but more context is needed to determine the actual relevance of the data and to input that into the information. In order to input data into the information, it is necessary to understand the relationships between the data and to see them in the appropriate context. This can be filled in on the basis of four questions: who, what, when and where. This is comparable to the series event-, fault-, and performance management.

Service interfaces

Characteristics of good service interfaces
The design of service interfaces is crucial for service management. The service interfaces meet the basic requirements of warranty, such as:
• The interfaces must be easy to find, and simple to use.
• The interfaces must be available and in a form that ensures opportunities for choice and flexibility for users.
• The interfaces must have sufficient capacity so that there is no waiting period if a large number of users try to make use of the interface simultaneously.
• The interfaces must accommodate users with varying skills, competencies, backgrounds and handicaps.

Combinations of service and technology
Advances in communication technology influence the interaction between service providers and their customers.

There are five ways in which technology contributes to communication with the customer:
1. **communication without technology** - such as with consulting services
2. **communication assisted by technology** - only the service provider has access to the technology; for example, an airport representative who uses a terminal to check in customers
3. **communication facilitated by technology** - both the customer and the provider have access to the same technology

4. **communication accomplished through technology** - service provider and customer are not in close proximity; for example, a customer who receives information via a service desk
5. **communication generated by technology** - the customer sees the service provider only in the form of technology, via a self-service interface; appropriate for routine activities, such as automated teller machines (ATMs)

Self-service channels
Automation is of added value to capacity. The capacity of channels for self-service has a low marginal cost, is infinitely scalable, does not get tired, offers unlimited consistent performances, and is available 24/7 for a relatively low cost.

Tools for the Service Strategy

Simulation
System dynamics is a methodology for understanding and managing the complex problems of IT organizations. It offers a way to get a handle on and to model feedback processes, supplies and flows, delays and other complex problems. It is a tool for evaluating the consequences of new policies and new structures before they are put into practice. System dynamics can provide insights into the following situations:
- **Capability trap** - In order to pressure the staff to work harder, the organization unconsciously sets the stage in which an increasingly higher level of tension is needed to arrive at the same level of performance.
- **Tool trap** - Although tools are often very useful, they also require the development of knowledge and experience; organizations overlook the impact of the increased short-term work pressure through training and learning and practical activities, and end up running additional unintended risks.
- **Fire-fighter trap** - When an organization rewards managers for putting out fires quickly, the performance can suffer over the long-term; in this case it might be better not to reward extinguishing fires.

Analytical modeling
There is a lot of depth and diversity in analytical modeling. The Service Strategy as well as other functions and processes in the Service Lifecycle can benefit from the knowledge that comes from analytical modeling for improving performance in light of technical, financial and time constraints. Six Sigma, PMBOK® and PRINCE2® offer well tested methods based on analytical models. They must be evaluated and adopted within the context of the Service Strategy and service management.

Return on investment

One of the greatest challenges in seeking financing for ITIL projects is identifying a specific business objective, which is dependent on service management. To that end, this section will cover the following three techniques:

- **business case** - a way of identifying business objectives that are dependent on service management
- **pre-program ROI** - techniques for quantitatively analyzing investments in service management
- **post-program ROI** - techniques for retroactively analyzing investments in service management

Business case

A way to justify investments in service management initiatives is to make a business case.

> A **business case** is a decision-making-, support-, and planning instrument that plans for the likely consequences of a business action.

The consequences can be qualitative as well as quantitative. A financial analysis is often central to a good business case. The business impact has to be directly linked to the business objectives. A business objective is the reason for considering a service management initiative. A strategic objective in the area of increasing productivity, for example, can be the introduction of competitive products. While a business case usually rests on a cost analysis, there are many other matters that are also important for a service management initiative.

Pre-program ROI

Capital budgeting is the investment of financing now in order to yield increasing cash inflows or decreasing cash outflows in the future. Capital budgeting decisions fall into two categories:

- **screening decisions** (**NPV**) - because you have to spend money to make money, the time value of money (discounted cash flow) plays a role; capital budgeting decisions can be based on analyses of the cash flows
- **preference decisions** (**IRR**) - decisions can also be based on preferential approaches

In this chapter, a distinction is made between two approaches: the Net Present Value (NPV) and the Internal Rate of Return (IRR). NPV is based on the comparison between cash inflows and cash outflows, where the difference, the "net present value", determines whether or not the investment is valuable. With IRR the yields over the entire lifecycle of a service are compared with the cash inflow (rate of return). Both approaches must decide if a proposed service management initiative will outlive a previously determined financial barrier (e.g. minimum return).

For service management programs, the NPV offers the following advantages over the IRR method:
• In general, NPV is easier to use.
• IRR accepts that the rate of return is, in fact, the rate of return of the program. This is a dubious assumption for environments with minimal experience with service management programs.

When NPV and IRR are not in agreement about the attractiveness of a project, then NPV is the best choice. NPV will make the more realistic assumption for the rate of return.

Post-program ROI
If a service management initiative is launched without prior ROI analysis, it is wise to do the analysis retroactively. The calculation of a service management ROI is illustrated in the basic model in Figure 3.18.

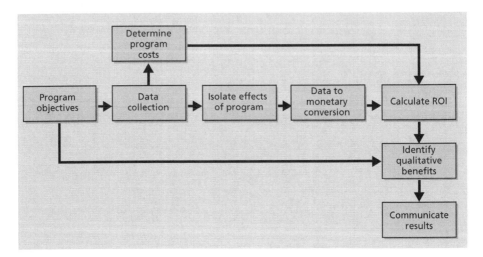

Figure 3.18 Post-program ROI approach

The Post-Program ROI approach comprises the following steps:

- **Program objectives** - Objectives must be clear because they convey the depth and scope of the ROI-analysis.
- **Data collection** - Examples include the metrics for the service quality, the transaction costs, customer satisfaction surveys, etc.
- **Isolation of the program's effects** - Various techniques are available to ensure that the program is effective; for example, the future analysis, which denotes what would have occurred if the program had not been started.
- **Monetary conversion of data** - In order to calculate the ROI, the data must be depicted as monetary values, so that the values can be compared with the costs.
- **Determining the program costs** - All of the related costs of the ITIL program are calculated (including, for example, planning, design, and implementation costs, technology costs, and training costs).
- **Calculate the ROI** - See the NPV - and IRR techniques in the previous sections.
- **Identify the qualitative benefits** - Qualitative benefits begin with how they are defined in the business case; the qualitative benefits are checked for a second time during the CSI phase.

Service delivery models and analysis

Organizations that analyze the existing methods for the delivery of services can make use of various models for the analysis:

- **Managed services** - The most traditional variant in which the business unit that needs the service handles the financing itself. This is the most expensive variant because the costs of the service are completely covered by the business unit.
- **Shared services** - Delivery of multiple services to one or more business unit through the collective use of infrastructures and resources. Cost savings through increased use of existing resources.
- **Utility-based services** - Maximizes the combination of delivered services over the same infrastructure so that even more services can be provided using the same resources. This is possible by providing services based on utility, depending on how much, how often and when the customer needs them. This model is the most cost-effective and the most refined because it requires a knowledge and capability level that most organizations do not have. These cost savings are possible through a deeper understanding of the architecture of the technology and the customers' needs, whereby a combination of services and architecture is achieved that makes maximum use of existing resources.
- **On-shore, off-shore, or near-shore?** - Determine what mix of on-shore, near-shore and off-shore services are right for a specific organization at a specific time. If an organization is not aware of its most important service cost components and the

dynamic of variable costs, then it will be difficult to make a logical and fact-based decision about outsourcing. The cost analysis of service delivery (service provisioning cost analysis) is the statistical estimation of the various forms of delivery and the determination of the most beneficial model.

- **Service provisioning cost analysis** - Statistically ranks the various forms of provisioning (and often providers) to determine the most beneficial model.

3.6 Implementation

From Strategy to Tactics and Production

Implementation based on the lifecycle
Strategic positions are converted into plans with objectives and ultimate goals, based on the lifecycle. Plans are a means for reaching these positions. Plans ensure that each phase in the Service Lifecycle have the capabilities and resources that are needed for achieving the strategic positions. The lifecycle provides the clarity and context for the development of the necessary capabilities and resources.

Plans translate the intentions of the strategy into actions, through Service Design, Service Transition, Service Operation, and CSI. The Service Strategy provides every phase of the lifecycle with input. CSI ensures that there is feedback by which the implementation of the strategy can be monitored during the entire lifecycle. (See Figure 3.19)

The Service Strategy defines the portfolio of services that are offered and the customers that are supported for a specific market.

Customers and service providers must both face the strategic risks that arise out of uncertainties. It is essential that risks be translated into opportunities and challenges, depending on the harmonization of service management capabilities with the existing needs of the customer. The Service Strategy needs CSI in order to guide the lifecycle elements to be certain that they have not missed any opportunities or challenges.

Patterns that emerge in implementing the Service Lifecycle ultimately lead to the assumption of new strategies. This bottom-up development of the Service Strategy, along with the traditional top-down approach, comprises a closed planning and management system for service strategies. This feedback- and learning process is an essential success factor for service management to make the necessary changes and innovations. (See Figure 3.20)

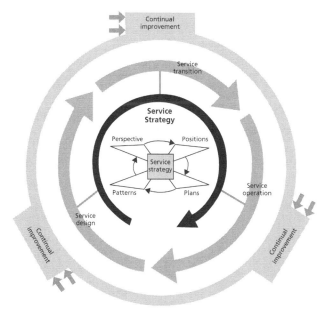

Figure 3.19 Strategy implemented in the Service Lifecycle

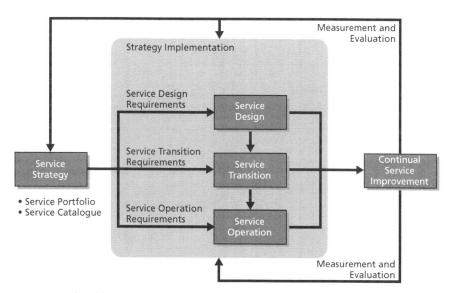

Figure 3.20 Closed-loop planning and monitoring system for strategy

Strategy and design

Service strategies arrive at implementation through the delivery and support of the Contract Portfolio in a specific market area. Contracts specify the terms and conditions under which value is provided to the customer through delivered services. Because every service is linked to one or more market area, the design of the service is related to the categories of customer assets and to the service models. They comprise the high-level input for the Service Design phase.

Service models

Factors from the utility and warranty that the customer wants influence the structure and dynamic of the models.

> **Service models** *describe how service assets interact with customer assets and create value for a given portfolio of contracts.*

The structure and dynamic have consequences for the Service Operation phase which are evaluated during the Service Transition phase.

Service models are developed by the market. (Figure 3.21)

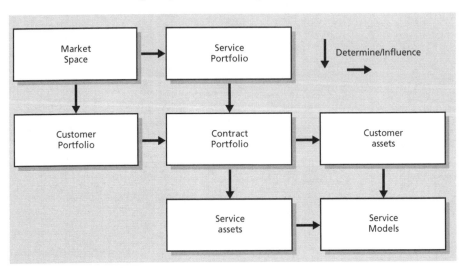

Figure 3.21 Service models are developed by the market

Outcome-oriented design
The attributes of a service constitute the characteristics that provide the service with form and function from the customer's perspective. It is a design challenge to determine which attributes must be adopted. Look at the business outcomes, for example, on the basis of the Kano model. A model developed by Noriaki Kano can be used to help understand customer preferences. The Kano Model considers attributes of an IT service grouped into areas such as Basic Factors, Excitement Factors, Performance Factors, etc.

Design focused on constraints
The development of a list of constraints and the visualization of the interaction requires a team of specialists from business and technology. They can observe and record the interaction among customers, providers, partners and advisors. All five phases of the Service Lifecycle provide input for those constraints. The method is a means for the Service Strategy to communicate the challenges and opportunities to the Service Design phase.

Strategy and transition
Service Strategy is dependent on the dynamic capabilities of service providers who make possible an effective response to the challenges and opportunities of customers and markets. Strategic plans always cost money. There are always costs and risks involved with decisions, such as introducing a new service, entering new market areas and serving new customers.

Service Transition represents one of the most important components of service management, with processes such as change management, configuration management and service deployment. The ability to carry out quick changes in service portfolios and contracts is a critical success factor in certain markets and strategies. Therefore the Service Transition is an important element in service management.

Strategy and operation
The ultimate achievement of strategies occurs in the operations phase. Therefore in developing strategies, it must always be kept in mind as to what is operationally feasible. Operations, on the other hand, must understand what kind of outcomes are needed in order to attain a particular strategy and must provide for adequate support.

Deployment patterns
Arrange service assets in patterns that are most effective in delivering value to the customer in every segment of the service catalogue. Deployment patterns in the Service Operation phase define the operational strategies for customers.

Hosting the contract portfolio

The need to provide service contracts influences the deployment patterns. Service contracts comprise the context in which the service portfolio provides services that are of value to the customer. Every contract represents the agreements that have been made with a customer regarding the utility and warranty of the services.

Hosting decisions require close coordination between Service Strategy and Service Operation. The strategy for a market influences the content of the customer portfolio and the service portfolio. Specific perspectives, positions, plans and patterns (the 4 Ps) determine the service offer, the associated contractual agreements and conditions, and the customers to whom they will be provided. The combination of service portfolios and the customer portfolio generates the contract portfolio.

Strategy and CSI

Quality perspective

Experience shows that SLA-metrics are necessary, but that they are not sufficient for measuring the quality of services that are provided to the customer. The quality of services, such as that experienced by customers, is based on the utility and warranty that are provided. Service quality depends on the positive impact of the service (utility) and the certainty of that impact (warranty).

The many definitions of quality can be summarized in four broad perspectives:
• level of excellence
• price-quality relationship
• conformity to specifications
• meeting or exceeding expectations

The most dominant perspective influences the assessment and management of services, especially in the context of service level management.

One of the most important decisions is the definition of the significance of service quality. Quality itself is a basis for strategies in a market. Therefore the definition of quality influences strategic decisions and objectives. It affects the design and the implementation of a service. It also influences the internal performance measures, policy and incentives that managers employ.

Warranty factors
There are differences and similarities in the methods of production of goods and services; how the value they create is transferred to the customer; how it is verified and how this certainty is established. Some factors are visible and measurable (tangible factors), while others are much more difficult to pin down (intangible factors).

Reliability
- **Applications and infrastructure** - In order to fulfill the warranty aspect of value to the customer, services must be reliable. This is essential input of the Service Strategy for Service Design and Service Operation. The provision of services with a high level of reliability can be the basis for strategic positioning. The reliability of a service depends on the reliability of the underlying service assets and their configuration. The reliability of an asset again depends on a variety of factors such as the quality of the design, development, installation, etc.
- **People and processes** - Reliability in terms of availability serves as an important factor for all service assets and infrastructures, as well as for people and processes. If support staff are not available, the service can ultimately fail as a result. The availability of all components, therefore, must also be managed. It is difficult to define the reliability and availability of people and processes. A factor, such as Mean Time Between Failures (MTBF), is much more difficult to calculate than hardware or network components. MTBF records the reliability of a service asset: the higher the MTBS, the higher the reliability.

Maintainability
Services must be quickly restored when they are unavailable to users. The Mean Time to Restore Service (MTRS) is the average recovery time within which a function (service, system or component) is operational again after a breakdown. The MTRS depends on several different factors, such as configuration of service assets, MTRS of individual components, the competence of support personnel, available resources, policy plans, procedures and redundancy.

Analyses of how the MTRS responds to each factor are useful for improving the performance and the design of services.

The MTRS can be reduced by reducing each of the components in the extended incident lifecycle (see Figure 3.22).

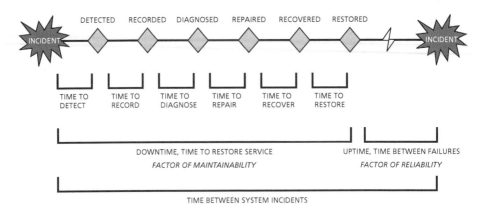

Figure 3.22 Improvement opportunities within the incident lifecycle

Redundancy

Redundancy is a way of increasing reliability and sustainability of systems. ITIL defines four redundancy types that can be used individually or in combination: Active and passive redundancy (for essential services), and diverse and homogeneous redundancy (for similar and specific service assets). This can be supported by various infrastructural methods that increase the accessibility of services.

Interactions between availability factors

The various factors that contribute to highly available services have a mutual effect on each other and can be managed together (See Figure 3.23).

Benefits, bottlenecks and risks

Complexity

IT organizations are complex systems. This explains why some service organizations are not inclined to change. Organizations are not always in a position to anticipate the long-term consequences of decisions and actions. This often results in their aversion to policy changes. Without continual learning processes, today's decisions often end up as tomorrow's problems.

A natural reaction is to divide services into processes that are managed by groups with specialized knowledge, experience and resources. This is fine as long as the mutual connection is not lost. Service management processes are a means, not an end.

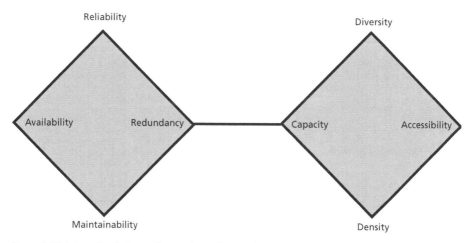

Figure 3.23 Interaction between factors that influence the availability of services

Coordination and control

The people who make the decisions often have limited time, attention and capacity. Therefore they delegate the roles and responsibilities to teams and individuals who are specialized in specific systems, processes, performances and results.

Service management is an interconnected set of specialized competencies that are defined around processes and lifecycle phases. An increase in the level of specialization leads to a requisite increase in coordination. Improved coordination is possible through the cooperation and monitoring between teams and individuals.

Problems with cooperation call for a way of connecting those groups with varying and possibly conflicting interests and objectives. This also applies to the cooperation between the service provider and the client.

Possible solutions:
- Make agreements in which everyone benefits.
- Maintain the shared views and agreed goals of service management; these are defined in service strategies, objectives, policy, rewards and incentives.
- Use collective processes that integrate groups and functions, shared applications that integrate the processes and shared infrastructures that integrate the applications.

Control perspectives are based on the objectives of one or more service management process or lifecycle phase. They help managers to focus on what is important and relevant to the processes that they control, and guarantee that high quality information is available to ensure effectiveness and efficiency.

Preserving Value

Deviations in performance

Mature customers are not only interested in the utility and warranty that they receive for the price they pay. They want to know the Total Cost of Utilization (TCU). The TCU concept is based on the principle of transaction costs. Customers see not only the costs of the actual consumption, but are also aware of all of the other related costs that are incurred indirectly during the process.

The creation of value for customers is a clearly visible objective for providers. The creation of value for their stakeholders is also of great importance. With Type I providers these two objectives are closely connected. With type III providers they can easily diverge or even conflict.

The exclusion of hidden costs is a challenge, a Critical Success Factor, and a risk.

Operational effectiveness and efficiency

Services must have a beneficial use from the perspective of both the customer and the service provider. This collective interest is essential to the economic feasibility of the services. Both the provider and the customer must, therefore, derive an economic value from the service.

Value is intangible and thus difficult to predict. Therefore efficiency must be created on the basis of a desired result. Effectiveness is the quality of being in a position to create a specific desired effect. In the context of service, the two effects are utility and warranty.

The increase of the efficiency of a process can result in the availability of extra capacity for other demands from the market, whereby the additional demand can be served with the same resources. Improvements in Service Design and Service Operation can drive this type of profit in efficiency. Thus, there is feedback and interaction between efficiency and desired effectiveness.

Increasing efficiency can lead to increasing effectiveness, which then can again lead to an increase in efficiency until a certain optimization limit has been reached.

Reducing hidden costs

One category of hidden costs includes transaction costs. These comprise, for example, resources that the provider supplies for determining the needs of the customer, the preferences of users, quality criteria and prices.

Standardization, shared services and reuse, coupled with segmentation and differentiated service levels can help recoup some of the transaction costs.

Confirmation of hidden benefits

Services offer an attractive alternative to the acquisition of assets. They offer the customer the utility of an asset while they can outsource the Maintenance and Repair Operations (MRO). MRO services belong to a separate category of services.

Standardization of service management processes for a specific industry leads to a higher level of efficiency and flexibility from consolidation, disaggregation, and flexible configuration of business processes, infrastructure components and human resources.

Effective use of intangible assets

Intangible assets are non-physical claims for future benefits generated through innovation, unique systems, processes, designs and competencies. The combination with tangible and financial assets ensures the creation of an economic value for the owner. Tangible assets include rival assets (or scarce assets): physical assets, human resources and financial assets. The specific use of this type of asset ensures that they cannot be used elsewhere. For example: people who assist the customer, equipment space, invested financial capital. Intangible assets, on the other hand, are not contentious because they are put in place simultaneously for different demands. The use of intangible assets, such as Web-based technologies and software-based automation of processes, can increase the scalability of service systems. Effective use of knowledge-intensive systems and processes is, in this respect, possible against virtual low costs.

From a service management perspective, the structure of service models, designs, and infrastructure can be analyzed in order to determine the ratio of intangible elements to tangible elements. Wherever possible, tangible elements should be replaced by intangibles so that the Service Design becomes scalable.

Measuring effectiveness

Measurements focus the organization on its strategic goals, follow the progression and provide the organization with feedback. Most IT organizations are good at monitoring data, but often they are not very good at providing insights into the effectiveness of the services that they offer. The "what" and the "where" can usually be answered accurately, while the "how" and the "why" are seen to be less important. It is crucial to perform the right analyses and to modify them as the strategy changes. In this case, organizations can apply the previously mentioned DIKW (Data-Information-Knowledge-Wisdom) knowledge management method.

Risks

The implementation of strategy leads to changes in the service portfolio. This then leads to the management of related risks. Decisions regarding risks must be balanced so that the potential benefits provide more value to the organization than the costs of addressing the risks. For example: innovation can be risky, but it can also result in greater benefits in the improvement of services.

For analysis purposes it can be useful to visualize the positive risk types that are related to opportunities, investments, and innovations in contrast to the negative risks such as failing to exploit opportunities, not succeeding in investing appropriately and ignoring innovation opportunities.

Definition of risk

ITIL defines risk as follows:

> **Risk** is an uncertain outcome, or in other words, a positive opportunity or a negative threat.

The task of risk management is to ensure that the organization makes use, in a cost-effective manner, of a risk framework that consists of a set of well-defined steps. (See Figure 3.24)

The goal is to support better decision-making through the use of a good understanding of the risks and their probable impact. There are two phases: risk analysis and risk management:

- **Risk analysis** - Risk analysis is involved with the gathering of information regarding the exposure to risks so that the organization makes the right decisions and oversees the risks in the appropriate the manner.
- **Risk management** - Risk management ensures that there are processes in place that are focused on monitoring risks, that reliable and current information about risks is available, that the right control balance for proceeding with the risks is applied,

Figure 3.24 Generic Framework for risk management

and that the decision-making is supported by a framework of risk analysis and evaluation.

Transfer of risks

Risk management plays a crucial role in service management (Figure 3.25). Services reduce the risk to the client's business, but they also bring risks to the service providers. Clients compensate service providers for these risks in a variety of ways: first and foremost by paying for the services (not possible with Type I).

Figure 3.25 Risk management plays an important role in service management

Service providers must ensure that sufficient compensation occurs but at the same time, they must remain reasonable. Costs are facts, but prices are a matter of policy. That means that certain investments, for example, can yield a profit over the course of time. In addition, with new services and customers, the risks can pay for themselves in the form of new customers (scale) or demand for other services (scope).

Supplements or changes to the client's portfolio must be preceded by an evaluation of the risks that the service provider is willing to assume on behalf of the client.

Risk analysis and risk management must be applied to the Service Pipeline and service catalogue in order to identify, curb and mitigate the risks within the lifecycle phases.

Risks for service providers
Risks for service providers arise when uncertainty from the customer's business is combined with uncertainties in their operations, and have an adverse effect across the lifecycle. It is useful to communicate risks in financial terms, which can be used as indicators instead of measures.

ITIL recognizes the following types of risks:
- **Contract risks** (a contract includes formally legal binding agreements between business and service providers) - Risks that the service provider will make it impossible to satisfy the contractual agreements are strategic risks, because they not only threaten the current production, but they also damage the trust for future interactions. The impact of contract risks and the underlying dangers and weaknesses may not be limited to just one specific function of the process. The customer makes no distinction between the source of risks. Coordination throughout the entire lifecycle is necessary in order to manage risks effectively.
- **Design risks** - Customers expect services to have a specific impact on the performance of their assets, which is a utility from their perspective. There is always a risk that the services will achieve undesired results. This is a performance risk. A poor performance is usually the result of a bad design.
- **Operational risks** - Every organization deals with operational risks. Viewed from a service management perspective, there are two types to distinguish: risks for the business units and risks for the service units.
- **Market risks** - Effective service management helps reduce the competitive risks by increasing the scale and scope of the demand for a service catalogue. Another approach is to modify the contents of the service catalogue so that customers can find the depth and breadth that they are looking for. Market risks can be reduced through:

- *Differentiation* - From the customer's perspective, assets that are scarce and complementary are interesting. Service providers can thus concentrate on providing the important assets that have not been provided by others. Un-served and underserved markets offer attractive opportunities.
- *Consolidation* - Consolidation of the demand reduces the financial risks for service providers as well as the operational risks for the customer.

CHAPTER 4

Introduction to Functions and Processes

4.1 Introduction

Processes are *internal* affairs for the IT service provider. An organization that is still trying to gain control of its processes therefore has an **internal focus**. Organizations that focus on gaining control of their systems in order to provide services are still internally focused. The organization is not ready for an **external focus** until it controls its services and is able to vary them on request. This external focus is required to evolve into that desirable customer-focused organization.

Because organizations can be in different stages of maturity, IT managers require a broad orientation in their discipline. Most organizations are now working on the introduction of a process-focused or customer-focused approach, or still have to start working on this. Process control is therefore a vital step on the road towards a **mature customer-focused organization**.

ITIL has made an important contribution to the organization of that process-focused operating method in the past decade. The development started in North-western Europe and has made some progress on most other continents in the last few years also. On a global scale, however, a minimal number of organizations have actually started with this approach - and an even smaller number have made serious progress at this point. The organization change projects that were thought to be necessary to convert to a process-focused organization were not all successful.

These findings lead us to conclude that the majority of organizations in the world require access to good information and best practices concerning the **business processes of**

IT organizations. Fortunately, that information is abundant. The ITIL version 2 books provide comprehensive documentation on the most important processes, while ITIL version 3 adds even more information.

The **process model** is at least as important as the processes because processes must be deployed in the right relationships to achieve the desired effect of a process-focused approach. There are many different process models available. The experiences gained with these processes and process models in recent years have been documented comprehensively in books, magazines and white papers, and have been presented at countless conventions.

4.2 Management of processes

Every organization aims to realize its vision, mission, strategy, objectives and policies, which means that appropriate activities have to be undertaken.

For example, a restaurant will have to purchase fresh ingredients, the chefs will have to work together to provide consistent results, and there should be no major differences in style among the waiting staff. A restaurant will only be awarded a three-star rating when it manages to provide the same high quality over an extended period of time. This is not always the case: there will be changes among the waiting staff, a successful approach may not last, and chefs often leave to open their own restaurants. Providing consistently high quality means that the component activities have to be coordinated: the better and more efficiently the kitchen operates, the higher the quality of service that can be provided to the guests.

In the example of the restaurant, appropriate activities include buying vegetables, bookkeeping, ordering publicity material, receiving guests, cleaning tables, peeling potatoes and making coffee. With just such an unstructured list, something will be left out and staff will easily become confused. It is therefore a better idea to structure the activities. Preferably these will be structured in such a way as to allow us to see how each group of activities contributes to the objectives of the business, and how they are related to other activities.

Such groups of activities are known as **processes**. If the process structure of an organization is clearly described, it will show:
- what has to be done
- what the expected inputs and results are
- how we measure whether the processes deliver the expected results
- how the results of one process affect those of another process

Processes can be defined in many ways. Depending upon the objectives of the creator, more or less emphasis will be on specific aspects. For example, a highly detailed process description will allow for a high level of control. Superficial process definitions will illustrate that the creator does not care much about the way in which the steps are executed.

Once the processes are defined, the roles, responsibilities and people can be assigned to specific aspects, bringing the process to the level of a *procedure*.

Processes

When arranging activities into processes, we do not use the existing allocation of tasks, nor the existing departmental divisions. This is a conscious choice. By opting for a process structure, it often becomes evident that certain activities in the organization are uncoordinated, duplicated, neglected or unnecessary.

> A **process** is a structured set of activities designed to accomplish a defined objective.

Instead, we look at the **objective** of the process and the **relationships** with other processes. A process is a series of activities carried out to convert input into an output, and ultimately into an outcome. The **input** is concerned with the resources being used in the process. The (reported) **output** describes the immediate results of the process, while the **outcome** indicates the long-term results of the process (in terms of meaningful effect). Through **control** activities, we can associate the input and output of each of the processes with **policies and standards** to provide information about the results to be obtained by the process. Control regulates the input and the **throughput** in case the throughput or output parameters are not compliant with these standards and policies. This produces chains of processes that show the input that goes into the organization and what the result, and it also monitors points in the chains in order to check the quality of the products and services provided by the organization.

The standards for the output of each process have to be defined, in such a way that the complete chain of processes in the process model meets the corporate objective. If the output of a process meets the defined requirements, then the process is **effective** in transforming its input into its output. To be really effective, the outcome should be taken into consideration rather than merely focusing on the output. If the activities in the process are also carried out with the minimum required effort and cost, then the process is **efficient**. It is the task of process management to use **planning and control** to ensure that processes are executed in an effective and efficient way.

We can study each process separately to optimize its quality. The **process owner** is responsible for the process results. The **process manager** is responsible for the realization and structure of the process, and reports to the process owner.

The logical combination of activities results in clear transfer points where the quality of processes can be monitored. In the restaurant example, we can separate responsibility for purchasing and cooking, so that the chefs do not have to purchase anything and can concentrate on their core activities.

The management of the organization can provide control on the basis of the process quality of the process as demonstrated by data from the results of each process. In most cases, the relevant **performance indicators** and standards will already be agreed upon. In this case the process manager can do the day-to-day control of the process. The process owner will assess the results based on a **report** of performance indicators and checks whether the results meet the agreed standard. Without clear indicators, it would be difficult for a process owner to determine whether the process is under control, and if planned improvements are being implemented.

Processes are often described using **procedures** and **work instructions**.

> A ***procedure*** *is a specified way to carry out an activity or a process.*
> *A procedure describes the "how", and can also describe "who" carries the*
> *activities out. A procedure may include stages from different processes. A*
> *procedure can vary depending on the organization.*
>
> *A set of **work instructions** defines how one or more activities in a procedure should*
> *be carried out in detail, using technology or other resources.*

A process is defined as a logically related series of activities executed to meet the goals of a defined objective. Processes are composed of two kinds of activities: the activities to realize the goal (operational activities concerned with the throughput), and the activities to manage these (control activities). The control activities make sure the operational activities (the workflow) are performed in time, in the right order, etc. (For example, in the processing of changes it is always ensured that a test is performed *before* a release is taken into production and not *afterwards*.)

Processes and departments

Most businesses are hierarchically organized. There are departments that are responsible for the activities of a group of employees. There are various ways of structuring departments, such as by customer, product, region or discipline. IT services generally depend on several departments, customers or disciplines. For example, if there is an IT service to provide users with access to an accounting program on a central computer, this will involve several disciplines. The computer center has to make the program and database accessible, the data and telecommunications department has to make the computer center accessible, and the PC support team has to provide users with an interface to access the application.

Processes that span several departments (teams) can monitor the quality of a service by monitoring particular aspects of quality, such as availability, capacity, cost and stability. A service organization will try to match these quality aspects with the customer's demands. The structure of such processes can ensure that good information is available about the provision of services, so that the planning and control of services can be improved.

Figure 4.1 shows a basic example of the combinations of activities in a process (indicated by the dashed lines).

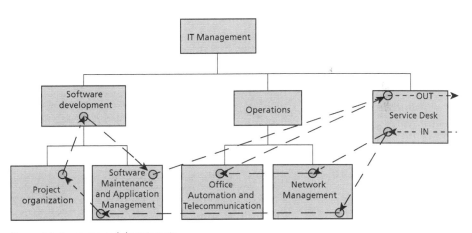

Figure 4.1 Processes and departments

IT service management and processes

IT service management has been known as the process and service-focused approach of what was initially known as Information Technology management. The shift of management from infrastructure to processes has paved the way for the term IT service management as a process and customer-focused discipline. Processes should always have a defined objective. The objective of IT service management processes is to contribute to the quality of the IT services. Quality management and process control are part of the organization and its policies.

By using a process approach, best practices for IT service management describe how services can be delivered, using the most effective and efficient series of activities. The Service Lifecycle in ITIL V3 is based on these process descriptions. The structure and allocation of tasks and responsibilities between functions and departments depends on the type of organization, and these structures vary widely among IT departments, and they often change. The description of the process structure however, provides a common point of reference that changes less rapidly. This can help to maintain the quality of IT services during and after reorganizations, and also among service providers and partners as they change. This makes service providers far less sensitive to organizational change, and much more flexible: providers can continually adapt their organization to changing conditions, leaving the core of their processes in place. In this way the shop can stay open during reconstruction work. However, reality may pose some practical problems, making this more difficult in practice than it seems in theory.

Applying the best process definitions of the industry allows IT service providers to concentrate on their business. As with other fields of industry, the processes in the IT industry are similar for all organizations of the same nature. Many of the process descriptions documented in ITIL have been recognized as the best that the industry could hope to adopt.

4.3 Teams, roles and positions in ITSM

Organizations divide the various tasks for carrying out processes or activities in many different ways. Tasks can be covered by organizational bodies, such as groups, teams, departments or divisions. These organizational bodies are then managed in **hierarchical organizations** by a line manager, who has a certain "span of control" and who manages one or more of these bodies. **Flat organizations** have relatively few layers in this hierarchy. Organizations can also divide the tasks more in the spirit of equality, such as, for example, **network organizations**, in which the cooperation between the various bodies is paramount.

Besides hierarchical organizations, which manage through "the line", there are also **project organizations**, which manage primarily by using temporary forms of project cooperation, while **process organizations** are managed primarily by means of an agreed work method. Obviously, these types of management can be combined in innumerable ways. As a result of this, we are seeing a great number of unique organizational configurations in the field.

Organizations can distinguish themselves from other organizations, particularly in respect to the type of organization they operate. An organization that is directed toward hierarchy will have a staff primarily of senior line management. A process-oriented organization will have staff that are responsible for processes. Depending on the degree to which management is based on processes, the line or projects, the staff will consist of a mix of the relevant responsible managers.

When setting up an organization, positions and roles are also used, in addition to the various groups (teams, departments, divisions). **Roles** are sets of responsibilities, activities and authorities granted to a person or team. One person or team may have multiple roles; for example, the roles of Configuration Manager and Change Manager may be carried out by a single person. **Positions** (functions) are traditionally recognized as tasks and responsibilities that are assigned to a specific person. A person in a particular position has a clearly defined package of tasks and responsibilities which may include various roles. Positions can also be more broadly defined as a logical concept that refers to the people and automated measures that carry out a clearly defined process, an activity or a combination of processes or activities.

4.4 Tools used in ITSM

In the performance of tasks in IT service management, innumerable automated support aids can be used: these are referred to as tools. With the help of these tools, management tasks can be automated; for example, monitoring tasks or software distribution tasks. Other tools support the performance of the activities themselves; for example, service desk tools or service management tools. The latter category, in fact, supports the management of several processes and are therefore often referred to as workflow tools - although they may not have actual workflow engines.

The fact that the IT field is fundamentally focused on automated facilities (for information processing) has led to a virtual deluge of tools appearing on the market, which have greatly increased the performance capacity of IT organizations.

4.5 Communication in IT service organizations

People, process, partners and technology provide the main "machinery" of any organization, but they only work well if the machine is oiled: **communication** is an essential element in any organization. If the people do not know about the processes or use the wrong instructions or tools, the output may not be as anticipated.

People are core assets of the organization. This is not only due to the fact that they need to be in place to perform certain activities or to take decisions, but also because people have the good habit of communicating. When an organization applies highly detailed instructions for all its activities, it will end up in a bureaucracy. On the other hand, an organization without any rules is will most likely end up in chaos. Whichever balance an organization is trying to find here, it will always benefit enormously from communication between the people in the organization. A regular and formal meeting culture will support this, but organizations should not underestimate the important role of informal communication: many projects have been saved by means of a simple chat in the tea room, or in the car park.

Formal structures on communication include:
- **reporting** - internal and external reporting, aimed at management or customers, project progress reports, alerts
- **meetings** - formal project meetings, regular meetings with specific targets
- **online facilities** - email systems, chat-rooms, pagers, groupware, document sharing systems, messenger facilities, teleconferencing and virtual meeting facilities
- **notice boards** - near the coffee maker, water cooler, at the entrance of the building, in the company restaurant

IT teams and departments, as well as users, internal customers and service production teams, must communicate with each other. The **stakeholders** for communication can thus be found among all managers and employees who are involved in service management, in all the layers of the organization, and with all customers, users and service providers. Good communication can prevent problems. All communication must have a particular goal or result. Every team, process and every department must have a clear **communications policy**.

IT service management includes several types of communication, such as:
- routine operational communication
- communication between teams
- performance reports
- communication during projects

- communication when there are changes
- communication in case of exceptions
- communication in case of emergencies
- training for new or adapted processes and service designs
- communication with service production teams regarding service strategies and design

4.6 Culture

Organizations that want to change, for example to improve the quality of their services, will eventually be confronted with the current organizational culture and will have to deal with any changes to this culture as a consequence of the overall change. The organizational culture, or corporate culture, refers to the way in which people deal with each other in the organization; the way in which decisions are made and implemented; and the attitude of employees to their work, customers, service providers, superiors and colleagues.

Culture, which depends on the standards and values of the people in the organization, cannot be controlled, but it can be influenced. Influencing the culture of an organization requires leadership in the form of a clear and consistent policy, as well as a supportive personnel policy.

The corporate culture can have a major influence on the provision of IT services. Businesses value innovation in different ways. In a stable organization, where the culture places little value on innovation, it will be difficult to adjust its IT services in line with changes in the organization of the customer. If the IT department is unstable, then a culture which values change can pose a serious threat to the quality of its services. In that case, a "free for all" culture can develop where many uncontrolled changes lead to a large number of faults.

4.7 Processes, projects, programs and portfolios

Activities can be managed from a process perspective, from an organizational hierarchy (line) perspective, from a project perspective, or from any combination of these three. Organizations that tend to apply just one of these management systems often miss the benefits of the others. The practical choice often depends upon history, culture, available skills and competences, and personal preferences. The optimum choice may be entirely different, but the requirements for applying this optimum may be hard to realize and vary in time.

There are no "hard and fast laws" for the way an organization should combine processes, projects and programs. However, it is generally accepted that there are some consequences attached to modern practices in IT service organizations, since the most widely accepted approach to service management is based on process management. This means that whenever the organization works with projects or programs, it should have established how these approaches work together.

The practical relationship between projects and processes is determined by the relative position of both in terms of "leading principles for the management of the organization": if projects are considered more important than processes, then decisions on projects will overrule decisions on processes; as a consequence, the organization will not be able to implement a stable set of processes. If it is the other way around, with projects only able to run within the constraints of agreed processes, then project management will be a discipline that will have to adapt to new boundaries and definitions (e.g. since projects always change something from A to B, they will most likely fall under the regime of Change, Release and Deployment Management).

The most suitable solution is dependent upon the understanding of the role of IT service management in the organization. To be able to find a solution for this management challenge, it is recommended that a common understanding of processes, projects, programs, and even portfolio's is created. The following definitions may be used:

- **Process** - A process is a structured set of activities designed to accomplish a defined objective.
- **Project** - A project is a temporary organization, with people and other assets required to achieve an objective.
- **Program** - A program consists of a number of projects and activities that are planned and managed together to achieve an overall set of related objectives.
- **Portfolio** - A portfolio is a set of projects and/or programs, which are not necessarily related, brought together for the sake of control, coordination and optimization of the portfolio in its totality. NB: In ITIL, a service portfolio is the complete set of services that are managed by a service provider.

Since the project/program/portfolio grouping is a hierarchical set of essential project resources, the issue can be downscaled to that of a relationship between a project and a process.

The most elementary difference between a process and a project is the one-off character of a project, versus the continuous character of the process. If a project has achieved its objectives, it means the end of the project. Processes can be run many times, both in parallel and in sequence. The nature of a process is aimed at its repeatable character:

processes are defined only in case of a repeatable string of activities that are important enough to be standardized and optimized.

Projects are aimed at changing a situation A into a situation B. This can involve a simple string of activities, but it can also be a very complex series of activities. Other elements of importance for projects include money, time, quality, organization and information. Project structures are normally used only if at least one of these elements is of considerable value.

Actually, projects are just ways of organizing a specific change in a situation. In that respect they have a resemblance with processes. It is often a matter of focus: processes focus at the specific sequence of activities, the decisions taken at certain milestone stages, and the quality of the activities involved. Processes are continuously instantiated and repeated, and use the same approach each time. Projects focus more at the time and money constraints, in terms of resources spent on the change and the projects end, and projects vary much more than processes.

A very practical way of combining the benefits of both management systems might be as follows:
- Processes set the scene for how specific series of activities are performed.
- Projects can be used to transform situation A into situation B, and always refer to a change.
- If the resources (time, money, or other) involved in a specific process require the level of attention that is normally applied in a project, then (part of) the process activities can be performed as a project, but always under the control of the process: if changes are performed, using project management techniques, the agreed change management policies still apply.

This would allow organizations to maintain a continuous customer focus and apply a process approach to optimize this customer focus, and at the same time benefit from the high level of resource control that can be achieved when using project management techniques.

4.8 Functions and processes in the lifecycle phases

For the sake of readability and uniformity, the following structure for the descriptions was used as much as possible:
- **introduction** - describes the purpose and aims of the process or function, its scope, value to the business, principles, guidelines, starting points and basic concepts

- **activities, methods and techniques** - explains the process or function in greater detail based on the workflow of activities (if possible); also describes commonly used methods and techniques
- **interfaces** - describes how the process or function is triggered, its inputs and outputs, and its links to other functions and processes
- **metrics** - describes the process metrics, in particular the Key Performance Indicators (KPIs)
- **implementation** - describes the Critical Success Factors (CSFs), challenges, risks and traps that may apply for the introduction of a process or function

Functions and Processes in Service Strategy

5.1 Financial Management

Introduction

Financial management is an integrated component of service management. It provides vital information that management need to ensure efficient and cost-effective service delivery. Efficient financial management enables the organization to provide a full justification of expenditures and allocate them directly to services.

IT organizations are increasingly aware of the fact that they are essentially equivalent to market-oriented organizations. Like the latter, IT organizations must understand and control the factors that influence demand. An IT organization also tries to reduce costs whilst improving its offering.

If implemented correctly, financial management generates meaningful and critical data on performance. It is also able to answer important organization issues, such as:
- Does our differentiation strategy result in higher profits and revenue, reduced costs or increased coverage?
- Which services cost most and why?
- Where are our greatest inefficiencies?

Financial management ensures that the costs of IT services are clear (e.g. via the service catalogue) and that the business understands them. The benefits are:
- improved decision-making
- speed of change
- service portfolio management
- financial compliance and control
- operational control
- value capture and creation

Service valuation
How can we achieve insight into the value creation process with the aid of financial management? Service valuation quantifies, in financial terms, the funding sought by the business and IT for service delivered, based on the agreed value of those services.

The main part of **service valuation** is to determine the value of services at a level the business considers realistic. This allows the provider to gain insight into which customer interests are served. An additional goal is improved management of demand and consumption behavior.

Translate utility and warranty to a monetary figure to calculate the value. ITIL defines two vital value concepts for service valuation:
- **Provisioning value** - The actual underlying costs to IT related to provisioning a service including all fulfillment elements, both tangible and intangible. These are costs like:
  - hardware and software license costs
  - annual maintenance costs for hardware and software
  - personnel that work to support or maintain a service
  - paid facilities
  - taxes, capital or interest charges
  - compliance costs
- **Service value potential** - The value-adding component based on the customer's perception of value from the service or expected marginal utility and warranty from using the service, in comparison with what is possible using the customers' own assets. Look at the service's individual value components to determine the true value of the service. Determine the eventual value of the service by adding these components and comparing them against the costs (provisioning value). Figure 5.1 shows the related concepts of value in greater detail.

Figure 5.1 Customer assets constitute the basis for value definition

Demand modeling
Inadequate management of service demand results in costs and risks. Demand modeling uses service-oriented financial information with factors of demand and supply in order to model anticipated usage by the business, and provisioning requirements of IT.

Service portfolio management
Financial management provides vital input for service portfolio management. By applying cost structures to services, companies can compare their service costs with those of other providers.

Service provisioning optimization
Financial management provides vital input for optimizing the service delivery (*Service Provisioning Optimization*, SPO). SPO investigates the financial inputs and constraints of service components or delivery models to determine if alternatives should be explored relating to how a service can be provisioned differently to make it more competitive in terms of cost or quality. It is this financial analysis of service components, constraints and value that is at the heart of financial management's interaction with service provisioning optimization.

Planning confidence

One objective of financial management is to ensure proper funding for delivery and consumption of services. Planning provides financial translation and qualification of expected future demand to IT services.

Planning can be split up into three primary areas. Each area represents financial results that are necessary to ensure continued visibility and service valuation:
- **operating & capital planning** (general and fixed asset ledgers) - translation of IT expenditures to collective financial systems as part of the collective planning cycle
- **demand planning** - need for and use of IT services as described earlier
- **regulatory and environmental planning** (compliance) - is controlled from the business

Careful planning results in confidence that the financial data and models provide accurate information on the development of service demand and offer.

Service investment analysis

Financial management provides the shared analytical models and knowledge to assess the expected value and/or return of a given initiative, solution, program or project in a standardized manner.

The objective of service investment analysis is to derive a value indication for the total lifecycle of a service based on (a) the value received and (b) costs incurred during the lifecycle of the service.

Accounting

Financial management plays a transitional role between corporate financial systems and service management. The results of a service-orientated accounting function is that far greater detail and understanding is achieved regarding service provisions and consumption, and the generation of data that feeds directly into the planning process.

Related functions and accounting properties are:
- **service recording** - assignment of a cost entry to the appropriate service
- **cost types** - high-level expenses categories such as hardware, software, labor, administration; once the basis for cost administration (e.g. per department, service or customer) is established, cost types are determined for cost entry; the number of cost types can vary depending on the organization's size; cost types must have a clear and recognisable description, so that costs can be easily allocated; the cost types can then be split up into *cost items*; settlement for each cost item may be established at a later stage

- **cost classification** - to ensure good cost control, it is important to gain insight into the types of costs that occur costs can be split up according to various aspects:
  - *Capital/operational costs:*
    - ◆ <u>Capital costs</u> have to do with the purchase of assets that generally last several years. The expenditure is written down over several years. Only the write-down amount is counted as costs.
    - ◆ <u>Operational costs</u> are costs that occur regularly and are not offset by tangible production assets (e.g. a maintenance contract for hardware, license costs, insurance premiums).
  - *Direct/indirect costs* - What costs contribute directly to a product or service and what costs do not:
    - ◆ <u>Direct costs</u> are costs that can be identified specifically and exclusively for an IT service. For instance activities and materials that are associated directly and exclusively with a specific service (e.g. a broadband connection).
    - ◆ <u>Indirect costs</u> cannot be identified directly for an IT service (e.g. facilities, supporting services and administrative costs).
  - *Fixed/variable costs* - Costs that vary or not with the production level:
    - ◆ <u>Fixed costs </u>are costs that do not vary due to production changes, such as investments in hardware, software and buildings. Generally the monthly or annual write-downs and interest are entered as costs instead of the acquisition costs. Fixed costs are ongoing, even if the service is reduced or terminated.
    - ◆ <u>Variable costs</u> are costs that do vary due to production changes, such as hiring external staff.
  - *Cost units* - The identified unit of consumption that is accounted for a particular service or service asset.

Variable Cost Dynamics (VCD)

Variable Cost Dynamics (VCD) focuses on analyzing and understanding the multitude of variables that impact service cost, how sensitive those elements are to variability, and the related incremental value changes that results. Among other benefits, VCD analysis can be used to identify a marginal change is unit cost resulting from adding or subtracting one or more incremental units of a service. This is helpful when applied toward the analysis of expected impacts from events such as acquisitions, divestitures, changes to the service portfolio or service provisioning alternatives etc.

Examples of variable service cost components are:
- number and type of users
- number of software licenses
- cost/operating footprint of data center

- delivery mechanisms
- number and type of resources
- cost of adding one more storage device
- costs of adding one more end user license

Activities, methods and techniques

Service valuation

During service valuation activities, the following decisions are made:

- **Direct costs versus indirect costs** - Can costs be attributed directly to a specific service or are they shared by several services (indirect costs)? Once the depth and breadth of the cost components are appropriately identified, rules or policy to guide how costs are to be spread among multiple services may be required.
- **Labor costs** - Develop a system to calculate the labor costs for a certain service.
- **Variable costs** - Include expenditures that are not fixed, but which vary depending on things such as the number of users or the number of running instances. To predict variable costs, you can use:
  - *Tiers* - identifying price breaks where plateaus occur within a provider so that customers are encouraged to obtain scale efficiencies familiar to the provider
  - *Maximum costs* - prescribing the cost of service based on the maximum level of variability
  - *Average costs* - this involves setting the cost of the service based on historical averaging of the variability.
- **Translation of cost account data to service value** - This is only possible once costs are attributed to service rather than, or in addition to, traditional cost accounts.

After having established the fixed and variable costs for each service, you need to think about the variable cost drivers and variation level of a service.

Funding model alternatives

This section summerizes several traditional models to fund IT services:

- **rolling plan funding** - a constant funding cycle; suitable for a Service Lifecycle for which a funding obligation is incurred at the start of a cycle and continues until changes occur or the lifecycle ends
- **trigger based plans** - critical triggers activate a planning for a specific event; the change management process, for instance, could act as a trigger for the planning process for all approved changes that have financial consequences
- **zero based funding** - funding only the actual costs to deliver an IT service

Business Impact Analysis (BIA)
A BIA seeks to identify an organizations most critical business services through an analysis of outage severity translated into a financial value, coupled with operational risk.

This information can help shape and improve operational performance. By enabling better decision making regarding prioritization of incident handling, problem management focus, change and release management operations, project priority and so on. It is a beneficial tool for identifying the costs of service failure and the relative worth of a service.
The cost of service outage is a financial value placed on a specific service and is meant to reflect the value of lost productivity and revenue over a specific period of time.

Key decisions for financial management
Some concepts in financial management have a big impact on the development of service strategies. ITIL highlights a number of these, allowing each organization to determine which the best alternatives are for its Service Strategy:
- **Cost recovery, value center, or accounting center?** - The IT financial cycle starts with funding applied to resources that create output. That output is identified as value by the customer, and this in turn induces the funding cycle to begin again. IT is typically referred to as a cost center, with funding based only on replenishing actual costs expended to deliver service.
- **Chargeback: to charge or not to charge?** - A chargeback model for IT can provide accountability and transparency. Charging costs increases the customer organization's awareness of the costs incurred to provide it with information. There are several chargeback models:
  - *notional charging* - an accounting method that provides insight into the costs that would be charged for a specific settlement method
  - *tiered subscription* - involves varying levels of warranty and/or utility offered for a service or service bundle, all of which have been priced, with the most appropriate chargeback models applied
  - *metered usage* - settling costs on the basis of carefully established consumption units; applies exclusively for organizations that have made serious progress in introducing financial management
  - *direct plus* - a more simplistic model where costs that can be attributed directly to a service are charged accordingly with some percentage of indirect costs shared amongst it
  - *fixed or user cost* - the simplest chargeback model in which the costs are divided on the basis of an agreed denominator, such as the number of users; this model contributes little to affecting customer behavior

- **Financial management implementation checklist** - A number of example implementation steps for phased implementation could include: plan, analyze, design, implement and measure.

5.2 Service Portfolio Management (SPM)

Introduction
A service portfolio describes the services of a provider in terms of business value. It articulates business needs and the service provider's response to those needs. Business values correspond to marketing terms; they assure that the competitiveness of the service provider is measurable with regard to the competitors.

With SPM, managers are better able to assess the quality requirements and accompanying costs. They can look for cost cutting action points, while at the same time maintaining the service quality.

> *Service Portfolio Management (SPM) is a dynamic method for governing investments in service management across the enterprise and managing them for value.*

The **goals** of service portfolio management are to realize and create maximum value, while at the same time keeping a lid on risks and costs.

SPM starts with documenting the standardized services of the organization and then those of the service catalogue. In order to be financially feasible, the portfolio must be a good mix of a service catalogue and services in pipeline.

The product manager plays an important role in the service portfolio management. He or she is responsible for managing services as a product during the entire lifecycle. Product managers coordinate and focus the organization and own the service catalogue. They work closely together with the Business Relationship Managers (BRM), who coordinate and focus on the client portfolio. In essence, SPM is a Governance method.

Value for the business
The service portfolio functions as basis of the decision-making framework. It helps answer the following strategic questions:
- Why should a customer buy these services?
- Why should a customer buy these services *from us?*
- What are the pricing and charge back models?
- What are our strengths and weaknesses, our priorities and our risks?
- How should our resources and capabilities be allocated?

- A service portfolio strategy gives the organization the capability to anticipate changes, while maintaining its strategy and planning.

Activities, methods and techniques

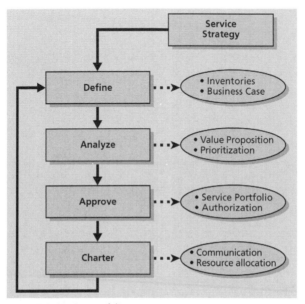

Figure 5.2 Service portfolio process

SPM is a dynamic and continuous process that entails the following work methods (see also Figure 5.2):

- **Defining** - Making an inventory of services, business cases and validating the portfolio data; start with collecting information on all *existing and proposed* services in order to determine the costs of the existing portfolio; the cyclic nature of the SPM process signifies that this phase does not only make the inventory of the services, but also validates the data over and over again; each service in the portfolio should have a business case.
- **Analyzing** - Maximizing the portfolio value, tuning, prioritizing and balancing supply and demand; in this phase, the strategic goals are given a concrete form. Start with a series of top/down questions such as:
  - What are the long-term goals of the service organization?
  - Which services are required to realize these goals?

- Which capabilities and resources are necessary to achieve those services? In other words, what are the four Ps?
- how will we get there?

The answers to these questions form the basis of the analysis, but also determine the desired result of SPM. Service investments must be subdivided into three strategic categories:

- *Run the Business (RTB)* - RTB investments concentrate on maintaining the service operations
- *Grow the Business (GTB)* - GTB investments are intended to expand the scope of services
- *Transform the Business (TTB)* - TTB investments are moves into new market spaces

- **Approving** - Finishing the proposed portfolio, authorizing services and resources and making decisions for the future; there are six different outcomes: retain, replace, rationalize, refactor, renew and retire.
- **Charter** - Communicating decisions, allocating resources and chartering services; start with a list of decisions and action items; communicate about this clearly and unequivocally with the organization; these decisions must be in tune with the budget decisions and financial plans; the expected value of each service must have been incorporated into the financial forecasts and resource planning; new services are promoted to Service Design existing services are refreshed in the service catalogue. Retired services begin their sunset to Service Transition.

With an efficient portfolio having optimal ROI and risk levels, an organization creates maximum value while using limited resources and capabilities.

5.3   Demand Management

Introduction

Challenges in managing service demand
Demand Management (DM) is a vital aspect of service management. It aligns supply with demand and aims to predict demand as closely as possible and, if possible, even regulate it. Badly managed demand represents a risk for service providers. Too much capacity, for instance, results in costs that do not yield value. Inadequate capacity, however, affects the service quality and limits service growth. Service Level Agreements (SLAs), demand prognosis, planning and strict coordination with the customer can reduce demand-related uncertainty, but they cannot eliminate it altogether.

Service management must deal with the additional problem of *synchronous production and consumption*. Service Operation is impossible without the existence of a demand that consumes the output. It is a pull-system, in which consumption cycles stimulate the production cycles (see Figure 5.3).

Figure 5.3   Close relationships between demand and capacity

Unlike goods, services cannot be manufactured in advance and stocked in a finished goods inventory in anticipation of demand. The productive capacity of resources available to a service is adjusted according to demand forecasts and patterns.

Activity-based demand management
Business processes are the primary source of demand for services. Patterns of Business Activity (PBAs) influence demand patterns as seen by the service providers (see Figure 5.4).

Figure 5.4 Business operations have an impact on demand patterns for services

It is extremely important to study the customer's business to identify, analyze and codify such patterns to provide sufficient basis for capacity management.

Activities, methods and techniques

Core services and supporting services
Core services deliver the basic outcomes desired by the customer. They represent the value that customers want and for which they are willing to pay. Core services anchor the value-proposition for the customer and provide a basis for their continued utilization and satisfaction. Supporting services either enable or enhance the value proposition. Enabling services are basic factors and enhancing services are excitement factors.

Developing a differentiated offering
The packing of core and supporting services is an essential aspect of market strategy. Service providers should thoroughly analyze the prevailing conditions in their business environment, the needs of the customer segments or types they serve, and the alternatives that are available to those customers. The decisions are strategic because they hold a long-term view for maintaining value for customers even as industry practices, norms, technologies and regulations change. Bundling of supporting services with core services has implications for the design and operation of services. Decisions have to made whether to standardize on the core or the supporting services.

Service providers must focus on the effective delivery of value through core services, whilst at the same time keeping an eye on the supporting services. Research has shown that customers are often dissatisfied with supporting services. Some supporting services, such as the service desk or technical support, are generally bundled but can also be offered separately. This is an important consideration in the strategic planning and review of the plans. These strategic decisions can have a major impact on the service provider's success at the portfolio level. They are important primarily to service providers who supply multiple organizations or business units (BUs) while at the same time being forced to reduce costs in order to preserve the competitiveness of their portfolio.

Services packages
ITIL defines a service packages as follows:

> A **service package** is a detailed description of an IT service that is available to be delivered to customers. A service package includes a Service Level Package (SLP) and one or more core services and supporting services.

The definition of a Service Level Package (SLP) is:

> A **Service Level Package (SLP)** is a defined level of utility and warranty for a particular Service Package. Each SLP is designed to meet the needs of a particular Pattern of Business Activity.

SLPs are associated with a set of service levels, a pricing policy, and a Core Service Package (CSP). ITIL defines a Core Service Package as follows:

> A **Core Service Package (CSP)** is a detailed description of a core service that may be shared by two or more Service Level Packages.

A Line of Service (LOS) is being defined as:

> A **Line of Service (LOS)** is a core service or supporting service that has multiple Service Level Packages. A Line of Service is managed by a Product Manager and each Service Level Package is designed to support a particular market segment.

Combinations of CSPs and SLPs are used to serve customer segments with differentiated values. CSP and SLP are loosely bundled to enable local optimization and maintain the service catalogue's efficiency as a whole (Figure 5.5).

Figure 5.5 SLPs are a way to deliver differentiated services

The advantage of CSPs is that they provide for strict control of core services used by all BUs. It controls complexity and assures the business outcome. Every BU can develop SLPs on the basis of applications and processes that serve their own market spaces.

Acronyms

AMIS	Availability Management Information System
APMG	APM Group
BCM	Business Continuity Management
BCP	Business Continuity Plan
BCS	British Computer Society
BIA	Business Impact Analysis
BPO	Business Process Outsourcing
BU	Business Unit
CAB	Change Advisory Board
CCM	Component Capacity Management
CFIA	Component Failure Impact Analysis
CI	Configuration Item
CMDB	Configuration Management Database
CMIS	Capacity Management Information System
CMS	Configuration Management System
CS	Change Schedule
CSF	Critical Success Factor
CSI	Continual Service Improvement
CSP	Core Service Package
DIKW	Data Information Knowledge Wisdom
DML	Definitive Media Library
ECAB	Emergency Change Advisory Board
ELS	Early Life Support
FTA	Fault Tree Analysis

HR	Human Resources
ISMS	Information Security Management System
ITIL	Information Technology Infrastructure Library
ITSCM	IT Service Continuity Management
itSMF	IT Service Management Forum
KEDB	Known Error Database
KPI	Key Performance Indicator
KPO	Knowledge Process Outsourcing
LCS	Loyalist Certification Services
LOS	Line of Service
M_o_R	Management of Risk
MTBF	Mean Time Between Failures
MTBSI	Mean Time Between Service Incidents
MTTR	Mean Time To Repair
MTRS	Mean Time to Restore Service
OGC	Office of Government Commerce
OLA	Operational Level Agreement
PBA	Pattern of Business Activity
PDCA	Plan Do Check Act
PFS	Prerequisites for Success
PIR	Post-Implementation Review
PRINCE2	PRojects IN Controlled Environments
PSA	Projected Service Availability
PSO	Projected Service Outage
RAD	Rapid Application Development
RFC	Request for Change
SAC	Service Acceptance Criteria
SACM	Service Asset and Configuration Management
SCD	Supplier and Contract Database
SCM	Service Catalogue Management
SDP	Service Design Package
SFA	Service Failure Analysis
SIP	Service Improvement Plan
SKMS	Service Knowledge Management System
SLA	Service Level Agreement
SLM	Service Level Management
SLP	Service Level Package
SLR	Service Level Requirement
SOC	Separation of Concerns

SPM	Service Portfolio Management
SPOC	Single Point of Contact
SPOF	Single Point of Failure
TCU	Total Cost of Utilization
TSO	The Stationary Office
UC	Underpinning Contract
VBF	Vital Business Function
VCD	Variable Cost Dynamics

Glossary

Where a term is relevant to a particular phase in the Lifecycle of an IT Service, or to one of the Core ITIL publications, this is indicated at the beginning of the definition. This glossary is based on the official ITIL V3 Glossary, version 01 of 30 May 2007.

Acceptance	Formal agreement that an IT Service, Process, Plan, or other Deliverable is complete, accurate, Reliable and meets its specified Requirements. Acceptance is usually preceded by Evaluation or Testing and is often required before proceeding to the next stage of a Project or Process. See Service Acceptance Criteria.
Access Management	(Service Operation) The Process responsible for allowing Users to make use of IT Services, data, or other Assets. Access Management helps to protect the Confidentiality, Integrity and Availability of Assets by ensuring that only authorized Users are able to access or modify the Assets. Access Management is sometimes referred to as Rights Management or Identity Management.
Account Manager	(Service Strategy) A Role that is very similar to Business Relationship Manager, but includes more commercial aspects. Most commonly used when dealing with External Customers.
Accounting	(Service Strategy) The Process responsible for identifying actual Costs of delivering IT Services, comparing these with budgeted costs, and managing variance from the Budget.
Accredited	Officially authorized to carry out a Role. For example an Accredited body may be authorized to provide training or to conduct Audits.
Active Monitoring	(Service Operation) Monitoring of a Configuration Item or an IT Service that uses automated regular checks to discover the current status. See Passive Monitoring.

Activity	A set of actions designed to achieve a particular result. Activities are usually defined as part of Processes or Plans, and are documented in Procedures.
Agreed Service Time	(Service Design) A synonym for Service Hours, commonly used in formal calculations of Availability. See Downtime.
Agreement	A Document that describes a formal understanding between two or more parties. An Agreement is not legally binding, unless it forms part of a Contract. See Service Level Agreement, Operational Level Agreement.
Alert	(Service Operation) A warning that a threshold has been reached, something has changed, or a Failure has occurred. Alerts are often created and managed by System Management tools and are managed by the Event Management Process.
Analytical Modeling	(Service Strategy) (Service Design) (Continual Service Improvement) A technique that uses mathematical Models to predict the behavior of a Configuration Item or IT Service. Analytical Models are commonly used in Capacity Management and Availability Management. See Modeling.
Application	Software that provides Functions that are required by an IT Service. Each Application may be part of more than one IT Service. An Application runs on one or more Servers or Clients. See Application Management, Application Portfolio.
Application Management	(Service Design) (Service Operation) The Function responsible for managing Applications throughout their Lifecycle.
Application Portfolio	(Service Design) A database or structured Document used to manage Applications throughout their Lifecycle. The Application Portfolio contains key Attributes of all Applications. The Application Portfolio is sometimes implemented as part of the Service Portfolio, or as part of the Configuration Management System.
Application Service Provider (ASP)	(Service Design) An External Service Provider that provides IT Services using Applications running at the Service Provider's premises. Users access the Applications by network connections to the Service Provider.
Application Sizing	(Service Design) The Activity responsible for understanding the Resource Requirements needed to support a new Application, or a major Change to an existing Application. Application Sizing helps to ensure that the IT Service can meet its agreed Service Level Targets for Capacity and Performance.
Architecture	(Service Design) The structure of a System or IT Service, including the Relationships of Components to each other and to the environment they are in. Architecture also includes the Standards and Guidelines which guide the design and evolution of the System.
Assembly	(Service Transition) A Configuration Item that is made up from a number of other CIs. For example a Server CI may contain CIs for CPUs, Disks, Memory etc.; an IT Service CI may contain many Hardware, Software and other CIs. See Component CI, Build.

Assessment	Inspection and analysis to check whether a Standard or set of Guidelines is being followed, that Records are accurate, or that Efficiency and Effectiveness targets are being met. See Audit.
Asset	(Service Strategy) Any Resource or Capability. Assets of a Service Provider include anything that could contribute to the delivery of a Service. Assets can be one of the following types: Management, Organization, Process, Knowledge, People, Information, Applications, Infrastructure, and Financial Capital.
Asset Management	(Service Transition) Asset Management is the Process responsible for tracking and reporting the value and ownership of financial Assets throughout their Lifecycle. Asset Management is part of an overall Service Asset and Configuration Management Process. See Asset Register.
Asset Register	(Service Transition) A list of Assets, which includes their ownership and value. The Asset Register is maintained by Asset Management.
Attribute	(Service Transition) A piece of information about a Configuration Item. Examples are name, location, Version number, and Cost. Attributes of CIs are recorded in the Configuration Management Database (CMDB). See Relationship.
Audit	Formal inspection and verification to check whether a Standard or set of Guidelines is being followed, that Records are accurate, or that Efficiency and Effectiveness targets are being met. An Audit may be carried out by internal or external groups. See Certification, Assessment.
Authority Matrix	Synonym for RACI.
Automatic Call Distribution (ACD)	(Service Operation) Use of Information Technology to direct an incoming telephone call to the most appropriate person in the shortest possible time. ACD is sometimes called Automated Call Distribution.
Availability	(Service Design) Ability of a Configuration Item or IT Service to perform its agreed Function when required. Availability is determined by Reliability, Maintainability, Serviceability, Performance, and Security. Availability is usually calculated as a percentage. This calculation is often based on Agreed Service Time and Downtime. It is Best Practice to calculate Availability using measurements of the Business output of the IT Service.
Availability Management	(Service Design) The Process responsible for defining, analyzing, Planning, measuring and improving all aspects of the Availability of IT Services. Availability Management is responsible for ensuring that all IT Infrastructure, Processes, Tools, Roles etc are appropriate for the agreed Service Level Targets for Availability.
Availability Management Information System (AMIS)	(Service Design) A virtual repository of all Availability Management data, usually stored in multiple physical locations. See Service Knowledge Management System.

Availability Plan	(Service Design) A Plan to ensure that existing and future Availability Requirements for IT Services can be provided Cost Effectively.
Back-out	Synonym for Remediation.
Backup	(Service Design) (Service Operation) Copying data to protect against loss of Integrity or Availability of the original.
Balanced Scorecard	(Continual Service Improvement) A management tool developed by Drs. Robert Kaplan (Harvard Business School) and David Norton. A Balanced Scorecard enables a Strategy to be broken down into Key Performance Indicators. Performance against the KPIs is used to demonstrate how well the Strategy is being achieved. A Balanced Scorecard has 4 major areas, each of which has a small number of KPIs. The same 4 areas are considered at different levels of detail throughout the Organization.
Baseline	(Continual Service Improvement) A Benchmark used as a reference point. For example: • An ITSM Baseline can be used as a starting point to measure the effect of a Service Improvement Plan • A Performance Baseline can be used to measure changes in Performance over the lifetime of an IT Service • A Configuration Management Baseline can be used to enable the IT Infrastructure to be restored to a known Configuration if a Change or Release fails
Benchmark	(Continual Service Improvement) The recorded state of something at a specific point in time. A Benchmark can be created for a Configuration, a Process, or any other set of data. For example, a benchmark can be used in: • Continual Service Improvement, to establish the current state for managing improvements. • Capacity Management, to document Performance characteristics during normal operations. • See Benchmarking, Baseline.
Benchmarking	(Continual Service Improvement) Comparing a Benchmark with a Baseline or with Best Practice. The term Benchmarking is also used to mean creating a series of Benchmarks over time, and comparing the results to measure progress or improvement.
Best Practice	Proven Activities or Processes that have been successfully used by multiple Organizations. ITIL is an example of Best Practice.
Brainstorming	(Service Design) A technique that helps a team to generate ideas. Ideas are not reviewed during the Brainstorming session, but at a later stage. Brainstorming is often used by Problem Management to identify possible causes.
British Standards Institution (BSI)	The UK National Standards body, responsible for creating and maintaining British Standards. See http://www.bsi-global.com for more information. See ISO.

Budget	A list of all the money an Organization or Business Unit plans to receive, and plans to pay out, over a specified period of time. See Budgeting, Planning.
Budgeting	The Activity of predicting and controlling the spending of money. Consists of a periodic negotiation cycle to set future Budgets (usually annual) and the day-to-day monitoring and adjusting of current Budgets.
Build	(Service Transition) The Activity of assembling a number of Configuration Items to create part of an IT Service. The term Build is also used to refer to a Release that is authorized for distribution. For example Server Build or laptop Build. See Configuration Baseline.
Build Environment	(Service Transition) A controlled Environment where Applications, IT Services and other Builds are assembled prior to being moved into a Test or Live Environment.
Business	(Service Strategy) An overall corporate entity or Organization formed of a number of Business Units. In the context of ITSM, the term Business includes public sector and not-for-profit organizations, as well as companies. An IT Service Provider provides IT Services to a Customer within a Business. The IT Service Provider may be part of the same Business as their Customer (Internal Service Provider), or part of another Business (External Service Provider).
Business Capacity Management (BCM)	(Service Design) In the context of ITSM, Business Capacity Management is the Activity responsible for understanding future Business Requirements for use in the Capacity Plan. See Service Capacity Management.
Business Case	(Service Strategy) Justification for a significant item of expenditure. Includes information about Costs, benefits, options, issues, Risks, and possible problems. See Cost Benefit Analysis.
Business Continuity Management (BCM)	(Service Design) The Business Process responsible for managing Risks that could seriously impact the Business. BCM safeguards the interests of key stakeholders, reputation, brand and value creating activities. The BCM Process involves reducing Risks to an acceptable level and planning for the recovery of Business Processes should a disruption to the Business occur. BCM sets the Objectives, Scope and Requirements for IT Service Continuity Management.
Business Continuity Plan (BCP)	(Service Design) A Plan defining the steps required to Restore Business Processes following a disruption. The Plan will also identify the triggers for Invocation, people to be involved, communications etc. IT Service Continuity Plans form a significant part of Business Continuity Plans.
Business Customer	(Service Strategy) A recipient of a product or a Service from the Business. For example if the Business is a car manufacturer then the Business Customer is someone who buys a car.

Business Impact Analysis (BIA)	(Service Strategy) BIA is the Activity in Business Continuity Management that identifies Vital Business Functions and their dependencies. These dependencies may include Suppliers, people, other Business Processes, IT Services etc. BIA defines the recovery requirements for IT Services. These requirements include Recovery Time Objectives, Recovery Point Objectives and minimum Service Level Targets for each IT Service.
Business Objective	(Service Strategy) The Objective of a Business Process, or of the Business as a whole. Business Objectives support the Business Vision, provide guidance for the IT Strategy, and are often supported by IT Services.
Business Operations	(Service Strategy) The day-to-day execution, monitoring and management of Business Processes.
Business Perspective	(Continual Service Improvement) An understanding of the Service Provider and IT Services from the point of view of the Business, and an understanding of the Business from the point of view of the Service Provider.
Business Process	A Process that is owned and carried out by the Business. A Business Process contributes to the delivery of a product or Service to a Business Customer. For example, a retailer may have a purchasing Process which helps to deliver Services to their Business Customers. Many Business Processes rely on IT Services.
Business Relationship Management	(Service Strategy) The Process or Function responsible for maintaining a Relationship with the Business. BRM usually includes: • Managing personal Relationships with Business managers • Providing input to Service Portfolio Management • Ensuring that the IT Service Provider is satisfying the Business needs of the Customers This Process has strong links with Service Level Management.
Business Relationship Manager (BRM)	(Service Strategy) A Role responsible for maintaining the Relationship with one or more Customers. This Role is often combined with the Service Level Manager Role. See Account Manager.
Business Service	An IT Service that directly supports a Business Process, as opposed to an Infrastructure Service which is used internally by the IT Service Provider and is not usually visible to the Business. The term Business Service is also used to mean a Service that is delivered to Business Customers by Business Units. For example delivery of financial services to Customers of a bank, or goods to the Customers of a retail store. Successful delivery of Business Services often depends on one or more IT Services.
Business Service Management (BSM)	(Service Strategy) (Service Design) An approach to the management of IT Services that considers the Business Processes supported and the Business value provided. This term also means the management of Business Services delivered to Business Customers.

Business Unit	(Service Strategy) A segment of the Business which has its own Plans, Metrics, income and Costs. Each Business Unit owns Assets and uses these to create value for Customers in the form of goods and Services.
Call	(Service Operation) A telephone call to the Service Desk from a User. A Call could result in an Incident or a Service Request being logged.
Call Centre	(Service Operation) An Organization or Business Unit which handles large numbers of incoming and outgoing telephone calls. See Service Desk.
Call Type	(Service Operation) A Category that is used to distinguish incoming requests to a Service Desk. Common Call Types are Incident, Service Request and Complaint.
Capability	(Service Strategy) The ability of an Organization, person, Process, Application, Configuration Item or IT Service to carry out an Activity. Capabilities are intangible Assets of an Organization. See Resource.
Capability Maturity Model (CMM)	(Continual Service Improvement) The Capability Maturity Model for Software (also known as the CMM and SW-CMM) is a model used to identify Best Practices to help increase Process Maturity. CMM was developed at the Software Engineering Institute (SEI) of Carnegie Mellon University. In 2000, the SW-CMM was upgraded to CMMI® (Capability Maturity Model Integration). The SEI no longer maintains the SW-CMM model, its associated appraisal methods, or training materials.
Capability Maturity Model Integration (CMMI)	(Continual Service Improvement) Capability Maturity Model® Integration (CMMI) is a process improvement approach developed by the Software Engineering Institute (SEI) of Carnegie Melon University. CMMI provides organizations with the essential elements of effective processes. It can be used to guide process improvement across a project, a division, or an entire organization. CMMI helps integrate traditionally separate organizational functions, set process improvement goals and priorities, provide guidance for quality processes, and provide a point of reference for appraising current processes. See http://www.sei.cmu.edu/cmmi/ for more information. See CMM, Continuous Improvement, Maturity.
Capacity	(Service Design) The maximum Throughput that a Configuration Item or IT Service can deliver whilst meeting agreed Service Level Targets. For some types of CI, Capacity may be the size or volume, for example a disk drive.
Capacity Management	(Service Design) The Process responsible for ensuring that the Capacity of IT Services and the IT Infrastructure is able to deliver agreed Service Level Targets in a Cost Effective and timely manner. Capacity Management considers all Resources required to deliver the IT Service, and plans for short, medium and long term Business Requirements.

Capacity Management Information System (CMIS)	(Service Design) A virtual repository of all Capacity Management data, usually stored in multiple physical locations. See Service Knowledge Management System.
Capacity Plan	(Service Design) A Capacity Plan is used to manage the Resources required to deliver IT Services. The Plan contains scenarios for different predictions of Business demand, and costed options to deliver the agreed Service Level Targets.
Capacity Planning	(Service Design) The Activity within Capacity Management responsible for creating a Capacity Plan.
Capital Expenditure (CAPEX)	(Service Strategy) The Cost of purchasing something that will become a financial Asset, for example computer equipment and buildings. The value of the Asset is Depreciated over multiple accounting periods.
Capital Item	(Service Strategy) An Asset that is of interest to Financial Management because it is above an agreed financial value.
Capitalization	(Service Strategy) Identifying major Cost as capital, even though no Asset is purchased. This is done to spread the impact of the Cost over multiple accounting periods. The most common example of this is software development, or purchase of a software license.
Category	A named group of things that have something in common. Categories are used to group similar things together. For example Cost Types are used to group similar types of Cost. Incident Categories are used to group similar types of Incident, CI Types are used to group similar types of Configuration Item.
Certification	Issuing a certificate to confirm Compliance to a Standard. Certification includes a formal Audit by an independent and Accredited body. The term Certification is also used to mean awarding a certificate to verify that a person has achieved a qualification.
Change	(Service Transition) The addition, modification or removal of anything that could have an effect on IT Services. The Scope should include all IT Services, Configuration Items, Processes, Documentation etc.
Change Advisory Board (CAB)	(Service Transition) A group of people that advises the Change Manager in the Assessment, prioritization and scheduling of Changes. This board is usually made up of representatives from all areas within the IT Service Provider, the Business, and Third Parties such as Suppliers.
Change Case	(Service Operation) A technique used to predict the impact of proposed Changes. Change Cases use specific scenarios to clarify the scope of proposed Changes and to help with Cost Benefit Analysis. See Use Case.

Change History	(Service Transition) Information about all changes made to a Configuration Item during its life. Change History consists of all those Change Records that apply to the CI.
Change Management	(Service Transition) The Process responsible for controlling the Lifecycle of all Changes. The primary objective of Change Management is to enable beneficial Changes to be made, with minimum disruption to IT Services.
Change Model	(Service Transition) A repeatable way of dealing with a particular Category of Change. A Change Model defines specific pre-defined steps that will be followed for a Change of this Category. Change Models may be very simple, with no requirement for approval (e.g. Password Reset) or may be very complex with many steps that require approval (e.g. major software Release). See Standard Change, Change Advisory Board.
Change Record	(Service Transition) A Record containing the details of a Change. Each Change Record documents the Lifecycle of a single Change. A Change Record is created for every Request for Change that is received, even those that are subsequently rejected. Change Records should reference the Configuration Items that are affected by the Change. Change Records are stored in the Configuration Management System.
Change Request	Synonym for Request for Change.
Change Schedule	(Service Transition) A Document that lists all approved Changes and their planned implementation dates. A Change Schedule is sometimes called a Forward Schedule of Change, even though it also contains information about Changes that have already been implemented.
Change Window	(Service Transition) A regular, agreed time when Changes or Releases may be implemented with minimal impact on Services. Change Windows are usually documented in SLAs.
Charging	(Service Strategy) Requiring payment for IT Services. Charging for IT Services is optional, and many Organizations choose to treat their IT Service Provider as a Cost Centre.
Chronological Analysis	(Service Operation) A technique used to help identify possible causes of Problems. All available data about the Problem is collected and sorted by date and time to provide a detailed timeline. This can make it possible to identify which Events may have been triggered by others.
CI Type	(Service Transition) A Category that is used to Classify CIs. The CI Type identifies the required Attributes and Relationships for a Configuration Record. Common CI Types include: hardware, Document, User etc.
Classification	The act of assigning a Category to something. Classification is used to ensure consistent management and reporting. CIs, Incidents, Problems, Changes etc. are usually classified.

Client	A generic term that means a Customer, the Business or a Business Customer. For example Client Manager may be used as a synonym for Account Manager. The term client is also used to mean:

- A computer that is used directly by a User, for example a PC, Handheld Computer, or Workstation.
- The part of a Client-Server Application that the User directly interfaces with. For example an email Client.

Closed	(Service Operation) The final Status in the Lifecycle of an Incident, Problem, Change etc. When the Status is Closed, no further action is taken.
Closure	(Service Operation) The act of changing the Status of an Incident, Problem, Change etc. to Closed.
COBIT	(Continual Service Improvement) Control Objectives for Information and related Technology (COBIT) provides guidance and Best Practice for the management of IT Processes. COBIT is published by the IT Governance Institute. See http://www.isaca.org/ for more information.
Code of Practice	A Guideline published by a public body or a Standards Organization, such as ISO or BSI. Many Standards consist of a Code of Practice and a Specification. The Code of Practice describes recommended Best Practice.
Cold Standby	Synonym for Gradual Recovery.
Commercial off the Shelf (COTS)	(Service Design) Application software or Middleware that can be purchased from a Third Party.
Compliance	Ensuring that a Standard or set of Guidelines is followed, or that proper, consistent accounting or other practices are being employed.
Component	A general term that is used to mean one part of something more complex. For example, a computer System may be a component of an IT Service, an Application may be a Component of a Release Unit. Components that need to be managed should be Configuration Items.
Component Capacity Management (CCM)	(Service Design) (Continual Service Improvement) The Process responsible for understanding the Capacity, Utilization, and Performance of Configuration Items. Data is collected, recorded and analyzed for use in the Capacity Plan. See Service Capacity Management.
Component CI	(Service Transition) A Configuration Item that is part of an Assembly. For example, a CPU or Memory CI may be part of a Server CI.
Component Failure Impact Analysis (CFIA)	(Service Design) A technique that helps to identify the impact of CI failure on IT Services. A matrix is created with IT Services on one edge and CIs on the other. This enables the identification of critical CIs (that could cause the failure of multiple IT Services) and of fragile IT Services (that have multiple Single Points of Failure).

Computer Telephony Integration (CTI)	(Service Operation) CTI is a general term covering any kind of integration between computers and telephone Systems. It is most commonly used to refer to Systems where an Application displays detailed screens relating to incoming or outgoing telephone calls. See Automatic Call Distribution, Interactive Voice Response.
Concurrency	A measure of the number of Users engaged in the same Operation at the same time.
Confidentiality	(Service Design) A security principle that requires that data should only be accessed by authorized people.
Configuration	(Service Transition) A generic term, used to describe a group of Configuration Items that work together to deliver an IT Service, or a recognizable part of an IT Service. Configuration is also used to describe the parameter settings for one or more CIs.
Configuration Baseline	(Service Transition) A Baseline of a Configuration that has been formally agreed and is managed through the Change Management process. A Configuration Baseline is used as a basis for future Builds, Releases and Changes.
Configuration Control	(Service Transition) The Activity responsible for ensuring that adding, modifying or removing a CI is properly managed, for example by submitting a Request for Change or Service Request.
Configuration Identification	(Service Transition) The Activity responsible for collecting information about Configuration Items and their Relationships, and loading this information into the CMDB. Configuration Identification is also responsible for labeling the CIs themselves, so that the corresponding Configuration Records can be found.
Configuration Item (CI)	(Service Transition) Any Component that needs to be managed in order to deliver an IT Service. Information about each CI is recorded in a Configuration Record within the Configuration Management System and is maintained throughout its Lifecycle by Configuration Management. CIs are under the control of Change Management. CIs typically include IT Services, hardware, software, buildings, people, and formal documentation such as Process documentation and SLAs.
Configuration Management	(Service Transition) The Process responsible for maintaining information about Configuration Items required to deliver an IT Service, including their Relationships. This information is managed throughout the Lifecycle of the CI. Configuration Management is part of an overall Service Asset and Configuration Management Process.
Configuration Management Database (CMDB)	(Service Transition) A database used to store Configuration Records throughout their Lifecycle. The Configuration Management System maintains one or more CMDBs, and each CMDB stores Attributes of CIs, and Relationships with other CIs.

Configuration Management System (CMS)	(Service Transition) A set of tools and databases that are used to manage an IT Service Provider's Configuration data. The CMS also includes information about Incidents, Problems, Known Errors, Changes and Releases; and may contain data about employees, Suppliers, locations, Business Units, Customers and Users. The CMS includes tools for collecting, storing, managing, updating, and presenting data about all Configuration Items and their Relationships. The CMS is maintained by Configuration Management and is used by all IT Service Management Processes. See Configuration Management Database, Service Knowledge Management System.
Configuration Record	(Service Transition) A Record containing the details of a Configuration Item. Each Configuration Record documents the Lifecycle of a single CI. Configuration Records are stored in a Configuration Management Database.
Configuration Structure	(Service Transition) The hierarchy and other Relationships between all the Configuration Items that comprise a Configuration.
Continual Service Improvement (CSI)	(Continual Service Improvement) A stage in the Lifecycle of an IT Service and the title of one of the Core ITIL publications. Continual Service Improvement is responsible for managing improvements to IT Service Management Processes and IT Services. The Performance of the IT Service Provider is continually measured and improvements are made to Processes, IT Services and IT Infrastructure in order to increase Efficiency, Effectiveness, and Cost Effectiveness. See Plan-Do-Check-Act.
Continuous Availability	(Service Design) An approach or design to achieve 100% Availability. A Continuously Available IT Service has no planned or unplanned Downtime.
Continuous Operation	(Service Design) An approach or design to eliminate planned Downtime of an IT Service. Note that individual Configuration Items may be down even though the IT Service is Available.
Contract	A legally binding Agreement between two or more parties.
Contract Portfolio	(Service Strategy) A database or structured Document used to manage Service Contracts or Agreements between an IT Service Provider and their Customers. Each IT Service delivered to a Customer should have a Contract or other Agreement which is listed in the Contract Portfolio. See Service Portfolio, Service Catalogue.
Control	A means of managing a Risk, ensuring that a Business Objective is achieved, or ensuring that a Process is followed. Example Controls include Policies, Procedures, Roles, RAID, door-locks etc. A control is sometimes called a Countermeasure or safeguard. Control also means to manage the utilization or behavior of a Configuration Item, System or IT Service.

Control Objectives for Information and related Technology (COBIT)	See COBIT.
Control perspective	(Service Strategy) An approach to the management of IT Services, Processes, Functions, Assets etc. There can be several different Control Perspectives on the same IT Service, Process etc., allowing different individuals or teams to focus on what is important and relevant to their specific Role. Example Control Perspectives include Reactive and Proactive management within IT Operations, or a Lifecycle view for an Application Project team.
Control Processes	The ISO/IEC 20000 Process group that includes Change Management and Configuration Management.
Core Service	(Service Strategy) An IT Service that delivers basic Outcomes desired by one or more Customers. See Supporting Service, Core Service Package.
Core Service Package (CSP)	(Service Strategy) A detailed description of a Core Service that may be shared by two or more Service Level Packages. See Service Package.
Cost	The amount of money spent on a specific Activity, IT Service, or Business Unit. Costs consist of real cost (money), notional cost such as people's time, and Depreciation.
Cost Benefit Analysis	An Activity that analyses and compares the Costs and the benefits involved in one or more alternative courses of action. See Business Case, Net Present Value, Internal Rate of Return, Return on Investment, Value on Investment.
Cost Centre	(Service Strategy) A Business Unit or Project to which Costs are assigned. A Cost Centre does not charge for Services provided. An IT Service Provider can be run as a Cost Centre or a Profit Centre.
Cost Effectiveness	A measure of the balance between the Effectiveness and Cost of a Service, Process or activity, A Cost Effective Process is one which achieves its Objectives at minimum Cost. See KPI, Return on Investment, Value for Money.
Cost Element	(Service Strategy) The middle level of category to which Costs are assigned in Budgeting and Accounting. The highest level category is Cost Type. For example a Cost Type of "people" could have cost elements of payroll, staff benefits, expenses, training, overtime etc. Cost Elements can be further broken down to give Cost Units. For example the Cost Element "expenses" could include Cost Units of Hotels, Transport, Meals etc.
Cost Management	(Service Strategy) A general term that is used to refer to Budgeting and Accounting, sometimes used as a synonym for Financial Management

Cost Type   (Service Strategy) The highest level of category to which Costs are assigned
                     in Budgeting and Accounting. For example hardware, software, people,
                     accommodation, external and Transfer.
                     See Cost Element, Cost Type.

Cost Unit   (Service Strategy) The lowest level of category to which Costs are assigned, Cost
                     Units are usually things that can be easily counted (e.g. staff numbers, software
                     licenses) or things easily measured (e.g. CPU usage, Electricity consumed).
                     Cost Units are included within Cost Elements. For example a Cost Element of
                     "expenses" could include Cost Units of Hotels, Transport, Meals etc.
                     See Cost Type.

Countermeasure   Can be used to refer to any type of Control. The term Countermeasure is most
                     often used when referring to measures that increase Resilience, Fault Tolerance or
                     Reliability of an IT Service.

Course Corrections   Changes made to a Plan or Activity that has already started, to ensure that it
                     will meet its Objectives. Course corrections are made as a result of Monitoring
                     progress.

CRAMM   A methodology and tool for analyzing and managing Risks. CRAMM was
                     developed by the UK Government, but is now privately owned. Further
                     information is available from http://www.cramm.com/

Crisis Management   The Process responsible for managing the wider implications of Business
                     Continuity. A Crisis Management team is responsible for Strategic issues such as
                     managing media relations and shareholder confidence, and decides when to invoke
                     Business Continuity Plans.

Critical Success   Something that must happen if a Process, Project, Plan, or IT Service is to succeed.
Factor (CSF)   KPIs are used to measure the achievement of each CSF. For example a CSF of
                     "protect IT Services when making Changes" could be measured by KPIs such
                     as "percentage reduction of unsuccessful Changes", "percentage reduction in
                     Changes causing Incidents" etc.

Culture   A set of values that is shared by a group of people, including expectations about
                     how people should behave, ideas, beliefs, and practices.
                     See Vision.

Customer   Someone who buys goods or Services. The Customer of an IT Service Provider is
                     the person or group who defines and agrees the Service Level Targets. The term
                     Customers is also sometimes informally used to mean Users, for example "this is a
                     Customer focused Organization".

Customer Portfolio   (Service Strategy) A database or structured Document used to record all
                     Customers of the IT Service Provider. The Customer Portfolio is the Business
                     Relationship Manager's view of the Customers who receive Services from the IT
                     Service Provider.
                     See Contract Portfolio, Service Portfolio.

Dashboard	(Service Operation) A graphical representation of overall IT Service Performance and Availability. Dashboard images may be updated in real-time, and can also be included in management reports and web pages. Dashboards can be used to support Service Level Management, Event Management or Incident Diagnosis.
Data-to-Information-to-Knowledge-to-Wisdom (DIKW)	A way of understanding the relationships between data, information, knowledge, and wisdom. DIKW shows how each of these builds on the others.
Definitive Media Library (DML)	(Service Transition) One or more locations in which the definitive and approved versions of all software Configuration Items are securely stored. The DML may also contain associated CIs such as licenses and documentation. The DML is a single logical storage area even if there are multiple locations. All software in the DML is under the control of Change and Release Management and is recorded in the Configuration Management System. Only software from the DML is acceptable for use in a Release.
Deliverable	Something that must be provided to meet a commitment in a Service Level Agreement or a Contract. Deliverable is also used in a more informal way to mean a planned output of any Process.
Demand Management	Activities that understand and influence Customer demand for Services and the provision of Capacity to meet these demands. At a Strategic level Demand Management can involve analysis of Patterns of Business Activity and User Profiles. At a Tactical level it can involve use of Differential Charging to encourage Customers to use IT Services at less busy times. See Capacity Management.
Deming Cycle	Synonym for Plan Do Check Act.
Dependency	The direct or indirect reliance of one Process or Activity upon another.
Deployment	(Service Transition) The Activity responsible for movement of new or changed hardware, software, documentation, Process, etc to the Live Environment. Deployment is part of the Release and Deployment Management Process. See Rollout.
Depreciation	(Service Strategy) A measure of the reduction in value of an Asset over its life. This is based on wearing out, consumption or other reduction in the useful economic value.
Design	(Service Design) An Activity or Process that identifies Requirements and then defines a solution that is able to meet these Requirements. See Service Design.
Detection	(Service Operation) A stage in the Incident Lifecycle. Detection results in the Incident becoming known to the Service Provider. Detection can be automatic, or can be the result of a User logging an Incident.

Development	(Service Design) The Process responsible for creating or modifying an IT Service or Application. Also used to mean the Role or group that carries out Development work.
Development Environment	(Service Design) An Environment used to create or modify IT Services or Applications. Development Environments are not typically subjected to the same degree of control as Test Environments or Live Environments. See Development.
Diagnosis	(Service Operation) A stage in the Incident and Problem Lifecycles. The purpose of Diagnosis is to identify a Workaround for an Incident or the Root Cause of a Problem.
Diagnostic Script	(Service Operation) A structured set of questions used by Service Desk staff to ensure they ask the correct questions, and to help them Classify, Resolve and assign Incidents. Diagnostic Scripts may also be made available to Users to help them diagnose and resolve their own Incidents.
Differential Charging	A technique used to support Demand Management by charging different amounts for the same IT Service Function at different times.
Direct Cost	(Service Strategy) A cost of providing an IT Service which can be allocated in full to a specific Customer, Cost Centre, Project etc. For example cost of providing non-shared servers or software licenses. See Indirect Cost.
Directory Service	(Service Operation) An Application that manages information about IT Infrastructure available on a network, and corresponding User access Rights.
Do Nothing	(Service Design) A Recovery Option. The Service Provider formally agrees with the Customer that Recovery of this IT Service will not be performed.
Document	Information in readable form. A Document may be paper or electronic. For example a Policy statement, Service Level Agreement, Incident Record, diagram of computer room layout. See Record.
Downtime	(Service Design) (Service Operation) The time when a Configuration Item or IT Service is not Available during its Agreed Service Time. The Availability of an IT Service is often calculated from Agreed Service Time and Downtime.
Driver	Something that influences Strategy, Objectives or Requirements. For example new legislation or the actions of competitors.
Early Life Support	(Service Transition) Support provided for a new or Changed IT Service for a period of time after it is Released. During Early Life Support the IT Service Provider may review the KPIs, Service Levels and Monitoring Thresholds, and provide additional Resources for Incident and Problem Management.

Economies of scale	(Service Strategy) The reduction in average Cost that is possible from increasing the usage of an IT Service or Asset. See Economies of Scope.
Economies of scope	(Service Strategy) The reduction in Cost that is allocated to an IT Service by using an existing Asset for an additional purpose. For example delivering a new IT Service from existing IT Infrastructure. See Economies of Scale.
Effectiveness	(Continual Service Improvement) A measure of whether the Objectives of a Process, Service or Activity have been achieved. An Effective Process or Activity is one that achieves its agreed Objectives. See KPI.
Efficiency	(Continual Service Improvement) A measure of whether the right amount of resources have been used to deliver a Process, Service or Activity. An Efficient Process achieves its Objectives with the minimum amount of time, money, people or other resources. See KPI.
Emergency Change	(Service Transition) A Change that must be introduced as soon as possible. For example to resolve a Major Incident or implement a Security patch. The Change Management Process will normally have a specific Procedure for handling Emergency Changes. See Emergency Change Advisory Board (ECAB).
Emergency Change Advisory Board (ECAB)	(Service Transition) A sub-set of the Change Advisory Board who make decisions about high impact Emergency Changes. Membership of the ECAB may be decided at the time a meeting is called, and depends on the nature of the Emergency Change.
Environment	(Service Transition) A subset of the IT Infrastructure that is used for a particular purpose. For Example: Live Environment, Test Environment, Build Environment. It is possible for multiple Environments to share a Configuration Item, for example Test and Live Environments may use different partitions on a single mainframe computer. Also used in the term Physical Environment to mean the accommodation, air conditioning, power system etc. Environment is also used as a generic term to mean the external conditions that influence or affect something.
Error	(Service Operation) A design flaw or malfunction that causes a Failure of one or more Configuration Items or IT Services. A mistake made by a person or a faulty Process that impacts a CI or IT Service is also an Error.
Escalation	(Service Operation) An Activity that obtains additional Resources when these are needed to meet Service Level Targets or Customer expectations. Escalation may be needed within any IT Service Management Process, but is most commonly associated with Incident Management, Problem Management and the management of Customer complaints. There are two types of Escalation, Functional Escalation and Hierarchic Escalation.

eSourcing Capability Model for Client Organizations (eSCM-CL)	(Service Strategy) A framework to help Organizations guide their analysis and decisions on Service Sourcing Models and Strategies. eSCM-CL was developed by Carnegie Mellon University. See eSCM-SP.
eSourcing Capability Model for Service Providers (eSCM-SP)	(Service Strategy) A framework to help IT Service Providers develop their IT Service Management Capabilities from a Service Sourcing perspective. eSCM-SP was developed by Carnegie Mellon University. See eSCM-CL.
Estimation	The use of experience to provide an approximate value for a Metric or Cost. Estimation is also used in Capacity and Availability Management as the cheapest and least accurate Modeling method.
Evaluation	(Service Transition) The Process responsible for assessing a new or Changed IT Service to ensure that Risks have been managed and to help determine whether to proceed with the Change. Evaluation is also used to mean comparing an actual Outcome with the intended Outcome, or comparing one alternative with another.
Event	(Service Operation) A change of state which has significance for the management of a Configuration Item or IT Service. The term Event is also used to mean an Alert or notification created by any IT Service, Configuration Item or Monitoring tool. Events typically require IT Operations personnel to take actions, and often lead to Incidents being logged.
Event Management	(Service Operation) The Process responsible for managing Events throughout their Lifecycle. Event Management is one of the main Activities of IT Operations.
Exception Report	A Document containing details of one or more KPIs or other important targets that have exceeded defined Thresholds. Examples include SLA targets being missed or about to be missed, and a Performance Metric indicating a potential Capacity problem.
Expanded Incident Lifecycle	(Availability Management) Detailed stages in the Lifecycle of an Incident. The stages are Detection, Diagnosis, Repair, Recovery, Restoration. The Expanded Incident Lifecycle is used to help understand all contributions to the Impact of Incidents and to Plan how these could be controlled or reduced.
External Customer	A Customer who works for a different Business to the IT Service Provider. See External Service Provider, Internal Customer.
External Metric	A Metric that is used to measure the delivery of IT Service to a Customer. External Metrics are usually defined in SLAs and reported to Customers. See Internal Metric.
External Service Provider	(Service Strategy) An IT Service Provider which is part of a different Organization to their Customer. An IT Service Provider may have both Internal Customers and External Customers. See Type III Service Provider.

External Sourcing	Synonym for Outsourcing.
Facilities Management	(Service Operation) The Function responsible for managing the physical Environment where the IT Infrastructure is located. Facilities Management includes all aspects of managing the physical Environment, for example power and cooling, building Access Management, and environmental Monitoring.
Failure	(Service Operation) Loss of ability to Operate to Specification, or to deliver the required output. The term Failure may be used when referring to IT Services, Processes, Activities, Configuration Items etc. A Failure often causes an Incident.
Failure Modes and Effects Analysis (FMEA)	An approach to assessing the potential Impact of Failures. FMEA involves analyzing what would happen after Failure of each Configuration Item, all the way up to the effect on the Business. FMEA is often used in Information Security Management and in IT Service Continuity Planning.
Fast Recovery	(Service Design) A Recovery Option which is also known as Hot Standby. Provision is made to Recover the IT Service in a short period of time, typically less than 24 hours. Fast Recovery typically uses a dedicated Fixed Facility with computer Systems, and software configured ready to run the IT Services. Immediate Recovery may take up to 24 hours if there is a need to Restore data from Backups.
Fault	Synonym for Error.
Fault Tolerance	(Service Design) The ability of an IT Service or Configuration Item to continue to Operate correctly after Failure of a Component part. See Resilience, Countermeasure.
Fault Tree Analysis (FTA)	(Service Design) (Continual Service Improvement) A technique that can be used to determine the chain of Events that leads to a Problem. Fault Tree Analysis represents a chain of Events using Boolean notation in a diagram.
Financial Management	(Service Strategy) The Function and Processes responsible for managing an IT Service Provider's Budgeting, Accounting and Charging Requirements.
First-line Support	(Service Operation) The first level in a hierarchy of Support Groups involved in the resolution of Incidents. Each level contains more specialist skills, or has more time or other Resources. See Escalation.
Fishbone Diagram	Synonym for Ishikawa Diagram.
Fit for Purpose	An informal term used to describe a Process, Configuration Item, IT Service etc. that is capable of meeting its Objectives or Service Levels. Being Fit for Purpose requires suitable Design, implementation, Control and maintenance.
Fixed Cost	(Service Strategy) A Cost that does not vary with IT Service usage. For example the cost of Server hardware. See Variable Cost.

Fixed Facility	(Service Design) A permanent building, available for use when needed by an IT Service Continuity Plan. See Recovery Option, Portable Facility.
Follow the Sun	(Service Operation) A methodology for using Service Desks and Support Groups around the world to provide seamless 24 * 7 Service. Calls, Incidents, Problems and Service Requests are passed between groups in different time zones.
Fulfilment	Performing Activities to meet a need or Requirement. For example by providing a new IT Service, or meeting a Service Request.
Function	A team or group of people and the tools they use to carry out one or more Processes or Activities. For example the Service Desk. The term Function also has two other meanings • An intended purpose of a Configuration Item, Person, Team, Process, or IT Service. For example one Function of an Email Service may be to store and forward outgoing mails, one Function of a Business Process may be to dispatch goods to Customers. • To perform the intended purpose correctly, "The computer is Functioning"
Functional Escalation	(Service Operation) Transferring an Incident, Problem or Change to a technical team with a higher level of expertise to assist in an Escalation.
Gap Analysis	(Continual Service Improvement) An Activity which compares two sets of data and identifies the differences. Gap Analysis is commonly used to compare a set of Requirements with actual delivery. See Benchmarking.
Governance	Ensuring that Policies and Strategy are actually implemented, and that required Processes are correctly followed. Governance includes defining Roles and responsibilities, measuring and reporting, and taking actions to resolve any issues identified.
Gradual Recovery	(Service Design) A Recovery Option which is also known as Cold Standby. Provision is made to Recover the IT Service in a period of time greater than 72 hours. Gradual Recovery typically uses a Portable or Fixed Facility that has environmental support and network cabling, but no computer Systems. The hardware and software are installed as part of the IT Service Continuity Plan.
Guideline	A Document describing Best Practice, that recommends what should be done. Compliance to a guideline is not normally enforced. See Standard.
Help Desk	(Service Operation) A point of contact for Users to log Incidents. A Help Desk is usually more technically focused than a Service Desk and does not provide a Single Point of Contact for all interaction. The term Help Desk is often used as a synonym for Service Desk.
Hierarchic Escalation	(Service Operation) Informing or involving more senior levels of management to assist in an Escalation.

High Availability	(Service Design) An approach or Design that minimizes or hides the effects of Configuration Item Failure on the Users of an IT Service. High Availability solutions are Designed to achieve an agreed level of Availability and make use of techniques such as Fault Tolerance, Resilience and fast Recovery to reduce the number of Incidents, and the Impact of Incidents.
Hot Standby	Synonym for Fast Recovery or Immediate Recovery.
Identity	(Service Operation) A unique name that is used to identify a User, person or Role. The Identity is used to grant Rights to that User, person, or Role. Example identities might be the username SmithJ or the Role "Change manager".
Immediate Recovery	(Service Design) A Recovery Option which is also known as Hot Standby. Provision is made to Recover the IT Service with no loss of Service. Immediate Recovery typically uses mirroring, load balancing and split site technologies.
Impact	(Service Operation) (Service Transition) A measure of the effect of an Incident, Problem or Change on Business Processes. Impact is often based on how Service Levels will be affected. Impact and Urgency are used to assign Priority.
Incident	(Service Operation) An unplanned interruption to an IT Service or a reduction in the Quality of an IT Service. Failure of a Configuration Item that has not yet impacted Service is also an Incident. For example Failure of one disk from a mirror set.
Incident Management	(Service Operation) The Process responsible for managing the Lifecycle of all Incidents. The primary Objective of Incident Management is to return the IT Service to Users as quickly as possible.
Incident Record	(Service Operation) A Record containing the details of an Incident. Each Incident record documents the Lifecycle of a single Incident.
Indirect Cost	(Service Strategy) A Cost of providing an IT Service which cannot be allocated in full to a specific Customer. For example Cost of providing shared Servers or software licenses. Also known as Overhead. See Direct Cost.
Information Security Management (ISM)	(Service Design) The Process that ensures the Confidentiality, Integrity and Availability of an Organization's Assets, information, data and IT Services. Information Security Management usually forms part of an Organizational approach to Security Management which has a wider scope than the IT Service Provider, and includes handling of paper, building access, phone calls etc., for the entire Organization.
Information Security Management System (ISMS)	(Service Design) The framework of Policy, Processes, Standards, Guidelines and tools that ensures an Organization can achieve its Information Security Management Objectives.
Information Security Policy	(Service Design) The Policy that governs the Organization's approach to Information Security Management.

Information Technology (IT)	The use of technology for the storage, communication or processing of information. The technology typically includes computers, telecommunications, Applications and other software. The information may include Business data, voice, images, video, etc. Information Technology is often used to support Business Processes through IT Services.
Infrastructure Service	An IT Service that is not directly used by the Business, but is required by the IT Service Provider so they can provide other IT Services. For example Directory Services, naming services, or communication services.
Insourcing	Synonym for Internal Sourcing.
Integrity	(Service Design) A security principle that ensures data and Configuration Items are only modified by authorized personnel and Activities. Integrity considers all possible causes of modification, including software and hardware Failure, environmental Events, and human intervention.
Interactive Voice Response (IVR)	(Service Operation) A form of Automatic Call Distribution that accepts User input, such as key presses and spoken commands, to identify the correct destination for incoming Calls.
Intermediate Recovery	(Service Design) A Recovery Option which is also known as Warm Standby. Provision is made to Recover the IT Service in a period of time between 24 and 72 hours. Intermediate Recovery typically uses a shared Portable or Fixed Facility that has computer Systems and network Components. The hardware and software will need to be configured, and data will need to be restored, as part of the IT Service Continuity Plan.
Internal Customer	A Customer who works for the same Business as the IT Service Provider. See Internal Service Provider, External Customer.
Internal Metric	A Metric that is used within the IT Service Provider to Monitor the Efficiency, Effectiveness or Cost Effectiveness of the IT Service Provider's internal Processes. Internal Metrics are not normally reported to the Customer of the IT Service. See External Metric.
Internal Rate of Return (IRR)	(Service Strategy) A technique used to help make decisions about Capital Expenditure. IRR calculates a figure that allows two or more alternative investments to be compared. A larger IRR indicates a better investment. See Net Present Value, Return on Investment.
Internal Service Provider	(Service Strategy) An IT Service Provider which is part of the same Organization as their Customer. An IT Service Provider may have both Internal Customers and External Customers. See Type I Service Provider, Type II Service Provider, Insource.
Internal Sourcing	(Service Strategy) Using an Internal Service Provider to manage IT Services. See Service Sourcing, Type I Service Provider, Type II Service Provider.

International Organization for Standardization (ISO)	The International Organization for Standardization (ISO) is the world's largest developer of Standards. ISO is a non-governmental organization which is a network of the national standards institutes of 156 countries. Further information about ISO is available from http://www.iso.org/
International Standards Organization	See International Organization for Standardization (ISO)
Internet Service Provider (ISP)	An External Service Provider that provides access to the Internet. Most ISPs also provide other IT Services such as web hosting.
Invocation	(Service Design) Initiation of the steps defined in a plan. For example initiating the IT Service Continuity Plan for one or more IT Services.
Ishikawa Diagram	(Service Operation) (Continual Service Improvement) A technique that helps a team to identify all the possible causes of a Problem. Originally devised by Kaoru Ishikawa, the output of this technique is a diagram that looks like a fishbone.
ISO 9000	A generic term that refers to a number of international Standards and Guidelines for Quality Management Systems. See http://www.iso.org/ for more information. See ISO.
ISO 9001	An international Standard for Quality Management Systems. See ISO 9000, Standard.
ISO/IEC 17799	(Continual Service Improvement) ISO Code of Practice for Information Security Management. See Standard.
ISO/IEC 20000	ISO Specification and Code of Practice for IT Service Management. ISO/IEC 20000 is aligned with ITIL Best Practice.
ISO/IEC 27001	(Service Design) (Continual Service Improvement) ISO Specification for Information Security Management. The corresponding Code of Practice is ISO/IEC 17799. See Standard.
IT Directorate	(Continual Service Improvement) Senior Management within a Service Provider, charged with developing and delivering IT services. Most commonly used in UK Government departments.
IT Infrastructure	All of the hardware, software, networks, facilities etc. that are required to Develop, Test, deliver, Monitor, Control or support IT Services. The term IT Infrastructure includes all of the Information Technology but not the associated people, Processes and documentation.
IT Operations	(Service Operation) Activities carried out by IT Operations Control, including Console Management, Job Scheduling, Backup and Restore, and Print and Output Management. IT Operations is also used as a synonym for Service Operation.

IT Operations Control	(Service Operation) The Function responsible for Monitoring and Control of the IT Services and IT Infrastructure. See Operations Bridge.
IT Operations Management	(Service Operation) The Function within an IT Service Provider which performs the daily Activities needed to manage IT Services and the supporting IT Infrastructure. IT Operations Management includes IT Operations Control and Facilities Management.
IT Service	A Service provided to one or more Customers by an IT Service Provider. An IT Service is based on the use of Information Technology and supports the Customer's Business Processes. An IT Service is made up from a combination of people, Processes and technology and should be defined in a Service Level Agreement.
IT Service Continuity Management (ITSCM)	(Service Design) The Process responsible for managing Risks that could seriously impact IT Services. ITSCM ensures that the IT Service Provider can always provide minimum agreed Service Levels, by reducing the Risk to an acceptable level and Planning for the Recovery of IT Services. ITSCM should be designed to support Business Continuity Management.
IT Service Continuity Plan	(Service Design) A Plan defining the steps required to Recover one or more IT Services. The Plan will also identify the triggers for Invocation, people to be involved, communications etc. The IT Service Continuity Plan should be part of a Business Continuity Plan.
IT Service Management (ITSM)	The implementation and management of Quality IT Services that meet the needs of the Business. IT Service Management is performed by IT Service Providers through an appropriate mix of people, Process and Information Technology. See Service Management.
IT Service Management Forum (itSMF)	The IT Service Management Forum is an independent Organization dedicated to promoting a professional approach to IT Service Management. The itSMF is a not-for-profit membership Organization with representation in many countries around the world (itSMF Chapters). The itSMF and its membership contribute to the development of ITIL and associated IT Service Management Standards. See http://www.itsmf.com/ for more information.
IT Service Provider	(Service Strategy) A Service Provider that provides IT Services to Internal Customers or External Customers.
IT Steering Group (ISG)	A formal group that is responsible for ensuring that Business and IT Service Provider Strategies and Plans are closely aligned. An IT Steering Group includes senior representatives from the Business and the IT Service Provider.
ITIL	A set of Best Practice guidance for IT Service Management. ITIL is owned by the OGC and consists of a series of publications giving guidance on the provision of Quality IT Services, and on the Processes and facilities needed to support them. See http://www.itil.co.uk/ for more information.

Job Description	A Document which defines the Roles, responsibilities, skills and knowledge required by a particular person. One Job Description can include multiple Roles, for example the Roles of Configuration Manager and Change Manager may be carried out by one person.
Job Scheduling	(Service Operation) Planning and managing the execution of software tasks that are required as part of an IT Service. Job Scheduling is carried out by IT Operations Management, and is often automated using software tools that run batch or online tasks at specific times of the day, week, month or year.
Kano Model	(Service Strategy) A Model developed by Noriaki Kano that is used to help understand Customer preferences. The Kano Model considers Attributes of an IT Service grouped into areas such as Basic Factors, Excitement Factors, Performance Factors etc.
Kepner & Tregoe Analysis	(Service Operation) (Continual Service Improvement) A structured approach to Problem solving. The Problem is analyzed in terms of what, where, when and extent. Possible causes are identified. The most probable cause is tested. The true cause is verified.
Key Performance Indicator (KPI)	(Continual Service Improvement) A Metric that is used to help manage a Process, IT Service or Activity. Many Metrics may be measured, but only the most important of these are defined as KPIs and used to actively manage and report on the Process, IT Service or Activity. KPIs should be selected to ensure that Efficiency, Effectiveness, and Cost Effectiveness are all managed. See Critical Success Factor.
Knowledge Base	(Service Transition) A logical database containing the data used by the Service Knowledge Management System.
Knowledge Management	(Service Transition) The Process responsible for gathering, analyzing, storing and sharing knowledge and information within an Organization. The primary purpose of Knowledge Management is to improve Efficiency by reducing the need to rediscover knowledge. See Data-to-Information-to-Knowledge-to-Wisdom, Service Knowledge Management System.
Known Error	(Service Operation) A Problem that has a documented Root Cause and a Workaround. Known Errors are created and managed throughout their Lifecycle by Problem Management. Known Errors may also be identified by Development or Suppliers.
Known Error Database (KEDB)	(Service Operation) A database containing all Known Error Records. This database is created by Problem Management and used by Incident and Problem Management. The Known Error Database is part of the Service Knowledge Management System.
Known Error Record	(Service Operation) A Record containing the details of a Known Error. Each Known Error Record documents the Lifecycle of a Known Error, including the Status, Root Cause and Workaround. In some implementations a Known Error is documented using additional fields in a Problem Record.

Lifecycle	The various stages in the life of an IT Service, Configuration Item, Incident, Problem, Change etc. The Lifecycle defines the Categories for Status and the Status transitions that are permitted. For example:

- The Lifecycle of an Application includes Requirements, Design, Build, Deploy, Operate, Optimize.
- The Expanded Incident Lifecycle includes Detect, Respond, Diagnose, Repair, Recover, Restore.
- The lifecycle of a Server may include: Ordered, Received, In Test, Live, Disposed etc.

Line of Service (LOS)	(Service Strategy) A Core Service or Supporting Service that has multiple Service Level Packages. A line of Service is managed by a Product Manager and each Service Level Package is designed to support a particular market segment.
Live	(Service Transition) Refers to an IT Service or Configuration Item that is being used to deliver Service to a Customer.
Live Environment	(Service Transition) A controlled Environment containing Live Configuration Items used to deliver IT Services to Customers.
Maintainability	(Service Design) A measure of how quickly and Effectively a Configuration Item or IT Service can be restored to normal working after a Failure. Maintainability is often measured and reported as MTRS. Maintainability is also used in the context of Software or IT Service Development to mean ability to be Changed or Repaired easily.
Major Incident	(Service Operation) The highest Category of Impact for an Incident. A Major Incident results in significant disruption to the Business.
Managed Services	(Service Strategy) A perspective on IT Services which emphasizes the fact that they are managed. The term Managed Services is also used as a synonym for Outsourced IT Services.
Management Information	Information that is used to support decision making by managers. Management Information is often generated automatically by tools supporting the various IT Service Management Processes. Management Information often includes the values of KPIs such as "Percentage of Changes leading to Incidents", or "first time fix rate".
Management of Risk (MoR)	The OGC methodology for managing Risks. MoR includes all the Activities required to identify and Control the exposure to Risk which may have an impact on the achievement of an Organization's Business Objectives. See http://www.m-o-r.org/ for more details.
Management System	The framework of Policy, Processes and Functions that ensures an Organization can achieve its Objectives.
Manual Workaround	A Workaround that requires manual intervention. Manual Workaround is also used as the name of a Recovery Option in which The Business Process Operates without the use of IT Services. This is a temporary measure and is usually combined with another Recovery Option.

Marginal Cost	(Service Strategy) The Cost of continuing to provide the IT Service. Marginal Cost does not include investment already made, for example the cost of developing new software and delivering training.
Market Space	(Service Strategy) All opportunities that an IT Service Provider could exploit to meet business needs of Customers. The Market Space identifies the possible IT Services that an IT Service Provider may wish to consider delivering.
Maturity	(Continual Service Improvement) A measure of the Reliability, Efficiency and Effectiveness of a Process, Function, Organization etc. The most mature Processes and Functions are formally aligned to Business Objectives and Strategy, and are supported by a framework for continual improvement.
Maturity Level	A named level in a Maturity model such as the Carnegie Mellon Capability Maturity Model Integration.
Mean Time Between Failures (MTBF)	(Service Design) A Metric for measuring and reporting Reliability. MTBF is the average time that a Configuration Item or IT Service can perform its agreed Function without interruption. This is measured from when the CI or IT Service starts working, until it next fails.
Mean Time Between Service Incidents (MTBSI)	(Service Design) A Metric used for measuring and reporting Reliability. MTBSI is the mean time from when a System or IT Service fails, until it next fails. MTBSI is equal to MTBF + MTRS.
Mean Time To Repair (MTTR)	The average time taken to repair a Configuration Item or IT Service after a Failure. MTTR is measured from when the CI or IT Service fails until it is Repaired. MTTR does not include the time required to Recover or Restore. MTTR is sometimes incorrectly used to mean Mean Time to Restore Service.
Mean Time to Restore Service (MTRS)	The average time taken to Restore a Configuration Item or IT Service after a Failure. MTRS is measured from when the CI or IT Service fails until it is fully Restored and delivering its normal functionality. See Maintainability, Mean Time to Repair.
Metric	(Continual Service Improvement) Something that is measured and reported to help manage a Process, IT Service or Activity. See KPI.
Middleware	(Service Design) Software that connects two or more software Components or Applications. Middleware is usually purchased from a Supplier, rather than developed within the IT Service Provider. See Off the Shelf.
Mission Statement	The Mission Statement of an Organization is a short but complete description of the overall purpose and intentions of that Organization. It states what is to be achieved, but not how this should be done.
Model	A representation of a System, Process, IT Service, Configuration Item etc. that is used to help understand or predict future behavior.

Modeling	A technique that is used to predict the future behavior of a System, Process, IT Service, Configuration Item etc. Modeling is commonly used in Financial Management, Capacity Management and Availability Management.
Monitor Control Loop	(Service Operation) Monitoring the output of a Task, Process, IT Service or Configuration Item; comparing this output to a predefined norm; and taking appropriate action based on this comparison.
Monitoring	(Service Operation) Repeated observation of a Configuration Item, IT Service or Process to detect Events and to ensure that the current status is known.
Near-Shore	(Service Strategy) Provision of Services from a country near the country where the Customer is based. This can be the provision of an IT Service, or of supporting Functions such as Service Desk. See On-shore, Off-shore.
Net Present Value (NPV)	(Service Strategy) A technique used to help make decisions about Capital Expenditure. NPV compares cash inflows to cash outflows. Positive NPV indicates that an investment is worthwhile. See Internal Rate of Return, Return on Investment.
Notional Charging	(Service Strategy) An approach to Charging for IT Services. Charges to Customers are calculated and Customers are informed of the charge, but no money is actually transferred. Notional Charging is sometimes introduced to ensure that Customers are aware of the Costs they incur, or as a stage during the introduction of real Charging.
Objective	The defined purpose or aim of a Process, an Activity or an Organization as a whole. Objectives are usually expressed as measurable targets. The term Objective is also informally used to mean a Requirement. See Outcome.
Off the Shelf	Synonym for Commercial Off the Shelf.
Office of Government Commerce (OGC)	OGC owns the ITIL brand (copyright and trademark). OGC is a UK Government department that supports the delivery of the government's procurement agenda through its work in collaborative procurement and in raising levels of procurement skills and capability with departments. It also provides support for complex public sector projects.
Office of Public Sector Information (OPSI)	OPSI license the Crown Copyright material used in the ITIL publications. They are a UK Government department who provide online access to UK legislation, license the re-use of Crown copyright material, manage the Information Fair Trader Scheme, maintain the Government's Information Asset Register and provide advice and guidance on official publishing and Crown copyright.
Off-shore	(Service Strategy) Provision of Services from a location outside the country where the Customer is based, often in a different continent. This can be the provision of an IT Service, or of supporting Functions such as Service Desk. See On-shore, Near-shore.

On-shore	(Service Strategy) Provision of Services from a location within the country where the Customer is based. See Off-shore, Near-shore.
Operate	To perform as expected. A Process or Configuration Item is said to Operate if it is delivering the Required outputs. Operate also means to perform one or more Operations. For example, to Operate a computer is to do the day-to-day Operations needed for it to perform as expected.
Operation	(Service Operation) Day-to-day management of an IT Service, System, or other Configuration Item. Operation is also used to mean any pre-defined Activity or Transaction. For example loading a magnetic tape, accepting money at a point of sale, or reading data from a disk drive.
Operational	The lowest of three levels of Planning and delivery (Strategic, Tactical, Operational). Operational Activities include the day-to-day or short term Planning or delivery of a Business Process or IT Service Management Process. The term Operational is also a synonym for Live.
Operational Cost	Cost resulting from running the IT Services. Often repeating payments. For example staff costs, hardware maintenance and electricity (also known as "current expenditure" or "revenue expenditure"). See Capital Expenditure.
Operational Expenditure (OPEX)	Synonym for Operational Cost.
Operational Level Agreement (OLA)	(Service Design) (Continual Service Improvement) An Agreement between an IT Service Provider and another part of the same Organization. An OLA supports the IT Service Provider's delivery of IT Services to Customers. The OLA defines the goods or Services to be provided and the responsibilities of both parties. For example there could be an OLA • between the IT Service Provider and a procurement department to obtain hardware in agreed times • between the Service Desk and a Support Group to provide Incident Resolution in agreed times. See Service Level Agreement.
Operations Bridge	(Service Operation) A physical location where IT Services and IT Infrastructure are monitored and managed.
Operations Control	Synonym for IT Operations Control.
Operations Management	Synonym for IT Operations Management.
Opportunity Cost	(Service Strategy) A Cost that is used in deciding between investment choices. Opportunity Cost represents the revenue that would have been generated by using the Resources in a different way. For example the Opportunity Cost of purchasing a new Server may include not carrying out a Service Improvement activity that the money could have been spent on. Opportunity cost analysis is used as part of a decision making processes, but is not treated as an actual Cost in any financial statement.

Optimize	Review, Plan and request Changes, in order to obtain the maximum Efficiency and Effectiveness from a Process, Configuration Item, Application etc.
Organization	A company, legal entity or other institution. Examples of Organizations that are not companies include International Standards Organization or itSMF. The term Organization is sometimes used to refer to any entity which has People, Resources and Budgets. For example a Project or Business Unit.
Outcome	The result of carrying out an Activity; following a Process; delivering an IT Service etc. The term Outcome is used to refer to intended results, as well as to actual results. See Objective.
Outsourcing	(Service Strategy) Using an External Service Provider to manage IT Services. See Service Sourcing, Type III Service Provider.
Overhead	Synonym for Indirect cost
Pain Value Analysis	(Service Operation) A technique used to help identify the Business Impact of one or more Problems. A formula is used to calculate Pain Value based on the number of Users affected, the duration of the Downtime, the Impact on each User, and the cost to the Business (if known).
Pareto Principle	(Service Operation) A technique used to priorities Activities. The Pareto Principle says that 80% of the value of any Activity is created with 20% of the effort. Pareto Analysis is also used in Problem Management to priorities possible Problem causes for investigation.
Partnership	A relationship between two Organizations which involves working closely together for common goals or mutual benefit. The IT Service Provider should have a Partnership with the Business, and with Third Parties who are critical to the delivery of IT Services. See Value Network.
Passive Monitoring	(Service Operation) Monitoring of a Configuration Item, an IT Service or a Process that relies on an Alert or notification to discover the current status. See Active Monitoring.
Pattern of Business Activity (PBA)	(Service Strategy) A Workload profile of one or more Business Activities. Patterns of Business Activity are used to help the IT Service Provider understand and plan for different levels of Business Activity. See User Profile.
Percentage utilization	(Service Design) The amount of time that a Component is busy over a given period of time. For example, if a CPU is busy for 1800 seconds in a one hour period, its utilization is 50%
Performance	A measure of what is achieved or delivered by a System, person, team, Process, or IT Service.

Performance Anatomy	(Service Strategy) An approach to Organizational Culture that integrates, and actively manages, leadership and strategy, people development, technology enablement, performance management and innovation.
Performance Management	(Continual Service Improvement) The Process responsible for day-to-day Capacity Management Activities. These include Monitoring, Threshold detection, Performance analysis and Tuning, and implementing Changes related to Performance and Capacity.
Pilot	(Service Transition) A limited Deployment of an IT Service, a Release or a Process to the Live Environment. A Pilot is used to reduce Risk and to gain User feedback and Acceptance. See Test, Evaluation.
Plan	A detailed proposal which describes the Activities and Resources needed to achieve an Objective. For example a Plan to implement a new IT Service or Process. ISO/IEC 20000 requires a Plan for the management of each IT Service Management Process.
Plan-Do-Check-Act	(Continual Service Improvement) A four stage cycle for Process management, attributed to Edward Deming. Plan-Do-Check-Act is also called the Deming Cycle. PLAN: Design or revise Processes that support the IT Services. DO: Implement the Plan and manage the Processes. CHECK: Measure the Processes and IT Services, compare with Objectives and produce reports ACT: Plan and implement Changes to improve the Processes.
Planned Downtime	(Service Design) Agreed time when an IT Service will not be available. Planned Downtime is often used for maintenance, upgrades and testing. See Change Window, Downtime.
Planning	An Activity responsible for creating one or more Plans. For example, Capacity Planning.
PMBOK	A Project management Standard maintained and published by the Project Management Institute. PMBOK stands for Project Management Body of Knowledge. See http://www.pmi.org/ for more information. See PRINCE2.
Policy	Formally documented management expectations and intentions. Policies are used to direct decisions, and to ensure consistent and appropriate development and implementation of Processes, Standards, Roles, Activities, IT Infrastructure etc.
Portable Facility	(Service Design) A prefabricated building, or a large vehicle, provided by a Third Party and moved to a site when needed by an IT Service Continuity Plan. See Recovery Option, Fixed Facility.
Post Implementation Review (PIR)	A Review that takes place after a Change or a Project has been implemented. A PIR determines if the Change or Project was successful, and identifies opportunities for improvement.

Practice	A way of working, or a way in which work must be done. Practices can include Activities, Processes, Functions, Standards and Guidelines. See Best Practice.
Prerequisite for Success (PFS)	An Activity that needs to be completed, or a condition that needs to be met, to enable successful implementation of a Plan or Process. A PFS is often an output from one Process that is a required input to another Process.
Pricing	(Service Strategy) The Activity for establishing how much Customers will be Charged.
PRINCE2	The standard UK government methodology for Project management. See http://www.ogc.gov.uk/prince2/ for more information. See PMBOK.
Priority	(Service Transition) (Service Operation) A Category used to identify the relative importance of an Incident, Problem or Change. Priority is based on Impact and Urgency, and is used to identify required times for actions to be taken. For example the SLA may state that Priority2 Incidents must be resolved within 12 hours.
Proactive Monitoring	(Service Operation) Monitoring that looks for patterns of Events to predict possible future Failures. See Reactive Monitoring.
Proactive Problem Management	(Service Operation) Part of the Problem Management Process. The Objective of Proactive Problem Management is to identify Problems that might otherwise be missed. Proactive Problem Management analyses Incident Records, and uses data collected by other IT Service Management Processes to identify trends or significant Problems.
Problem	(Service Operation) A cause of one or more Incidents. The cause is not usually known at the time a Problem Record is created, and the Problem Management Process is responsible for further investigation.
Problem Management	(Service Operation) The Process responsible for managing the Lifecycle of all Problems. The primary Objectives of Problem Management are to prevent Incidents from happening, and to minimize the Impact of Incidents that cannot be prevented.
Problem Record	(Service Operation) A Record containing the details of a Problem. Each Problem Record documents the Lifecycle of a single Problem.
Procedure	A Document containing steps that specify how to achieve an Activity. Procedures are defined as part of Processes. See Work Instruction.
Process	A structured set of Activities designed to accomplish a specific Objective. A Process takes one or more defined inputs and turns them into defined outputs. A Process may include any of the Roles, responsibilities, tools and management Controls required to reliably deliver the outputs. A Process may define Policies, Standards, Guidelines, Activities, and Work Instructions if they are needed.

Process Control	The Activity of planning and regulating a Process, with the Objective of performing the Process in an Effective, Efficient, and consistent manner.
Process Manager	A Role responsible for Operational management of a Process. The Process Manager's responsibilities include Planning and coordination of all Activities required to carry out, monitor and report on the Process. There may be several Process Managers for one Process, for example regional Change Managers or IT Service Continuity Managers for each data centre. The Process Manager Role is often assigned to the person who carries out the Process Owner Role, but the two Roles may be separate in larger Organizations.
Process Owner	A Role responsible for ensuring that a Process is Fit for Purpose. The Process Owner's responsibilities include sponsorship, Design, Change Management and continual improvement of the Process and its Metrics. This Role is often assigned to the same person who carries out the Process Manager Role, but the two Roles may be separate in larger Organizations.
Production Environment	Synonym for Live Environment.
Profit Centre	(Service Strategy) A Business Unit which charges for Services provided. A Profit Centre can be created with the objective of making a profit, recovering Costs, or running at a loss. An IT Service Provider can be run as a Cost Centre or a Profit Centre.
pro-forma	A template, or example Document containing example data that will be replaced with the real values when these are available.
Program	A number of Projects and Activities that are planned and managed together to achieve an overall set of related Objectives and other Outcomes.
Project	A temporary Organization, with people and other Assets required to achieve an Objective or other Outcome. Each Project has a Lifecycle that typically includes initiation, Planning, execution, Closure etc. Projects are usually managed using a formal methodology such as PRINCE2.
Projected Service Outage (PSO)	(Service Transition) A Document that identifies the effect of planned Changes, maintenance Activities and Test Plans on agreed Service Levels.
PRojects IN Controlled Environments (PRINCE2)	See PRINCE2.
Qualification	(Service Transition) An Activity that ensures that IT Infrastructure is appropriate, and correctly configured, to support an Application or IT Service. See Validation.

Quality	The ability of a product, Service, or Process to provide the intended value. For example, a hardware Component can be considered to be of high Quality if it performs as expected and delivers the required Reliability. Process Quality also requires an ability to monitor Effectiveness and Efficiency, and to improve them if necessary. See Quality Management System.
Quality Assurance (QA)	(Service Transition) The Process responsible for ensuring that the Quality of a product, Service or Process will provide its intended Value.
Quality Management System (QMS)	(Continual Service Improvement) The set of Processes responsible for ensuring that all work carried out by an Organization is of a suitable Quality to reliably meet Business Objectives or Service Levels. See ISO 9000.
Quick Win	(Continual Service Improvement) An improvement Activity which is expected to provide a Return on Investment in a short period of time with relatively small Cost and effort. See Pareto Principle.
RACI	(Service Design) (Continual Service Improvement) A Model used to help define Roles and Responsibilities. RACI stands for Responsible, Accountable, Consulted and Informed. See Stakeholder.
Reactive Monitoring	(Service Operation) Monitoring that takes action in response to an Event. For example submitting a batch job when the previous job completes, or logging an Incident when an Error occurs. See Proactive Monitoring.
Reciprocal Arrangement	(Service Design) A Recovery Option. An agreement between two Organizations to share resources in an emergency. For example, Computer Room space or use of a mainframe.
Record	A Document containing the results or other output from a Process or Activity. Records are evidence of the fact that an Activity took place and may be paper or electronic. For example, an Audit report, an Incident Record, or the minutes of a meeting.
Recovery	(Service Design) (Service Operation) Returning a Configuration Item or an IT Service to a working state. Recovery of an IT Service often includes recovering data to a known consistent state. After Recovery, further steps may be needed before the IT Service can be made available to the Users (Restoration).
Recovery Option	(Service Design) A Strategy for responding to an interruption to Service. Commonly used Strategies are Do Nothing, Manual Workaround, Reciprocal Arrangement, Gradual Recovery, Intermediate Recovery, Fast Recovery, Immediate Recovery. Recovery Options may make use of dedicated facilities, or Third Party facilities shared by multiple Businesses.

Recovery Point Objective (RPO)	(Service Operation) The maximum amount of data that may be lost when Service is Restored after an interruption. Recovery Point Objective is expressed as a length of time before the Failure. For example a Recovery Point Objective of one day may be supported by daily Backups, and up to 24 hours of data may be lost. Recovery Point Objectives for each IT Service should be negotiated, agreed and documented, and used as Requirements for Service Design and IT Service Continuity Plans.
Recovery Time Objective (RTO)	(Service Operation) The maximum time allowed for recovery of an IT Service following an interruption. The Service Level to be provided may be less than normal Service Level Targets. Recovery Time Objectives for each IT Service should be negotiated, agreed and documented. See Business Impact Analysis.
Redundancy	Synonym for Fault Tolerance. The term Redundant also has a generic meaning of obsolete, or no longer needed.
Relationship	A connection or interaction between two people or things. In Business Relationship Management it is the interaction between the IT Service Provider and the Business. In Configuration Management it is a link between two Configuration Items that identifies a dependency or connection between them. For example Applications may be linked to the Servers they run on, IT Services have many links to all the CIs that contribute to them.
Relationship Processes	The ISO/IEC 20000 Process group that includes Business Relationship Management and Supplier Management.
Release	(Service Transition) A collection of hardware, software, documentation, Processes or other Components required to implement one or more approved Changes to IT Services. The contents of each Release are managed, Tested, and Deployed as a single entity.
Release and Deployment Management	(Service Transition) The Process responsible for both Release Management and Deployment.
Release Identification	(Service Transition) A naming convention used to uniquely identify a Release. The Release Identification typically includes a reference to the Configuration Item and a version number. For example Microsoft Office 2003 SR2.
Release Management	(Service Transition) The Process responsible for Planning, scheduling and controlling the movement of Releases to Test and Live Environments. The primary Objective of Release Management is to ensure that the integrity of the Live Environment is protected and that the correct Components are released. Release Management is part of the Release and Deployment Management Process.
Release Process	The name used by ISO/IEC 20000 for the Process group that includes Release Management. This group does not include any other Processes. Release Process is also used as a synonym for Release Management Process.

Release Record   (Service Transition) A Record in the CMDB that defines the content of a Release.
                          A Release Record has Relationships with all Configuration Items that are affected
                          by the Release.

Release Unit   (Service Transition) Components of an IT Service that are normally Released
                          together. A Release Unit typically includes sufficient Components to perform a
                          useful Function. For example one Release Unit could be a Desktop PC, including
                          Hardware, Software, Licenses, Documentation etc. A different Release Unit may
                          be the complete Payroll Application, including IT Operations Procedures and User
                          training.

Release Window   Synonym for Change Window.

Reliability   (Service Design) (Continual Service Improvement) A measure of how long
                          a Configuration Item or IT Service can perform its agreed Function without
                          interruption. Usually measured as MTBF or MTBSI. The term Reliability can also
                          be used to state how likely it is that a Process, Function etc. will deliver its required
                          outputs.
                          See Availability.

Remediation   (Service Transition) Recovery to a known state after a failed Change or Release.

Repair   (Service Operation) The replacement or correction of a failed Configuration Item.

Request for Change   (Service Transition) A formal proposal for a Change to be made. An RFC includes
(RFC)   details of the proposed Change, and may be recorded on paper or electronically.
                          The term RFC is often misused to mean a Change Record, or the Change itself.

Request Fulfilment   (Service Operation) The Process responsible for managing the Lifecycle of all
                          Service Requests.

Requirement   (Service Design) A formal statement of what is needed. For example a Service
                          Level Requirement, a Project Requirement or the required Deliverables for a
                          Process.
                          See Statement of Requirements.

Resilience   (Service Design) The ability of a Configuration Item or IT Service to resist Failure
                          or to Recover quickly following a Failure. For example, an armored cable will resist
                          failure when put under stress.
                          See Fault Tolerance.

Resolution   (Service Operation) Action taken to repair the Root Cause of an Incident or
                          Problem, or to implement a Workaround.
                          In ISO/IEC 20000, Resolution Processes is the Process group that includes Incident
                          and Problem Management.

Resolution Processes   The ISO/IEC 20000 Process group that includes Incident Management and
                          Problem Management.

Resource	(Service Strategy) A generic term that includes IT Infrastructure, people, money or anything else that might help to deliver an IT Service. Resources are considered to be Assets of an Organization. See Capability, Service Asset.
Response Time	A measure of the time taken to complete an Operation or Transaction. Used in Capacity Management as a measure of IT Infrastructure Performance, and in Incident Management as a measure of the time taken to answer the phone, or to start Diagnosis.
Responsiveness	A measurement of the time taken to respond to something. This could be Response Time of a Transaction, or the speed with which an IT Service Provider responds to an Incident or Request for Change etc.
Restoration of Service	See Restore.
Restore	(Service Operation) Taking action to return an IT Service to the Users after Repair and Recovery from an Incident. This is the primary Objective of Incident Management.
Retire	(Service Transition) Permanent removal of an IT Service, or other Configuration Item, from the Live Environment. Retired is a stage in the Lifecycle of many Configuration Items.
Return on Investment (ROI)	(Service Strategy) (Continual Service Improvement) A measurement of the expected benefit of an investment. In the simplest sense it is the net profit of an investment divided by the net worth of the assets invested. See Net Present Value, Value on Investment.
Return to Normal	(Service Design) The phase of an IT Service Continuity Plan during which full normal operations are resumed. For example, if an alternate data centre has been in use, then this phase will bring the primary data centre back into operation, and restore the ability to invoke IT Service Continuity Plans again.
Review	An evaluation of a Change, Problem, Process, Project etc. Reviews are typically carried out at predefined points in the Lifecycle, and especially after Closure. The purpose of a Review is to ensure that all Deliverables have been provided, and to identify opportunities for improvement. See Post Implementation Review.
Rights	(Service Operation) Entitlements, or permissions, granted to a User or Role. For example the Right to modify particular data, or to authorize a Change.
Risk	A possible Event that could cause harm or loss, or affect the ability to achieve Objectives. A Risk is measured by the probability of a Threat, the Vulnerability of the Asset to that Threat, and the Impact it would have if it occurred.

Risk Assessment	The initial steps of Risk Management. Analyzing the value of Assets to the business, identifying Threats to those Assets, and evaluating how Vulnerable each Asset is to those Threats. Risk Assessment can be quantitative (based on numerical data) or qualitative.
Risk Management	The Process responsible for identifying, assessing and controlling Risks. See Risk Assessment.
Role	A set of responsibilities, Activities and authorities granted to a person or team. A Role is defined in a Process. One person or team may have multiple Roles, for example the Roles of Configuration Manager and Change Manager may be carried out by a single person.
Rollout	(Service Transition) Synonym for Deployment. Most often used to refer to complex or phased Deployments or Deployments to multiple locations.
Root Cause	(Service Operation) The underlying or original cause of an Incident or Problem.
Root Cause Analysis (RCA)	(Service Operation) An Activity that identifies the Root Cause of an Incident or Problem. RCA typically concentrates on IT Infrastructure failures. See Service Failure Analysis.
Running Costs	Synonym for Operational Costs
Scalability	The ability of an IT Service, Process, Configuration Item etc. to perform its agreed Function when the Workload or Scope changes.
Scope	The boundary, or extent, to which a Process, Procedure, Certification, Contract etc. applies. For example the Scope of Change Management may include all Live IT Services and related Configuration Items, the Scope of an ISO/IEC 20000 Certificate may include all IT Services delivered out of a named data centre.
Second-line Support	(Service Operation) The second level in a hierarchy of Support Groups involved in the resolution of Incidents and investigation of Problems. Each level contains more specialist skills, or has more time or other Resources.
Security	See Information Security Management
Security Management	Synonym for Information Security Management
Security Policy	Synonym for Information Security Policy
Separation of Concerns (SOC)	(Service Strategy) An approach to Designing a solution or IT Service that divides the problem into pieces that can be solved independently. This approach separates "what" is to be done from "how" it is to be done.
Server	(Service Operation) A computer that is connected to a network and provides software Functions that are used by other computers.
Service	A means of delivering value to Customers by facilitating Outcomes Customers want to achieve without the ownership of specific Costs and Risks.

Service Acceptance Criteria (SAC)	(Service Transition) A set of criteria used to ensure that an IT Service meets its functionality and Quality Requirements and that the IT Service Provider is ready to Operate the new IT Service when it has been Deployed. See Acceptance.
Service Analytics	(Service Strategy) A technique used in the Assessment of the Business Impact of Incidents. Service Analytics Models the dependencies between Configuration Items, and the dependencies of IT Services on Configuration Items.
Service Asset	Any Capability or Resource of a Service Provider. See Asset.
Service Asset and Configuration Management (SACM)	(Service Transition) The Process responsible for both Configuration Management and Asset Management.
Service Capacity Management (SCM)	(Service Design) (Continual Service Improvement) The Activity responsible for understanding the Performance and Capacity of IT Services. The Resources used by each IT Service and the pattern of usage over time are collected, recorded, and analyzed for use in the Capacity Plan. See Business Capacity Management, Component Capacity Management.
Service Catalogue	(Service Design) A database or structured Document with information about all Live IT Services, including those available for Deployment. The Service Catalogue is the only part of the Service Portfolio published to Customers, and is used to support the sale and delivery of IT Services. The Service Catalogue includes information about deliverables, prices, contact points, ordering and request Processes. See Contract Portfolio.
Service Continuity Management	Synonym for IT Service Continuity Management.
Service Contract	(Service Strategy) A Contract to deliver one or more IT Services. The term Service Contract is also used to mean any Agreement to deliver IT Services, whether this is a legal Contract or an SLA. See Contract Portfolio.
Service Culture	A Customer oriented Culture. The major Objectives of a Service Culture are Customer satisfaction and helping the Customer to achieve their Business Objectives.
Service Design	(Service Design) A stage in the Lifecycle of an IT Service. Service Design includes a number of Processes and Functions and is the title of one of the Core ITIL publications. See Design.
Service Design Package	(Service Design) Document(s) defining all aspects of an IT Service and its Requirements through each stage of its Lifecycle. A Service Design Package is produced for each new IT Service, major Change, or IT Service Retirement.

Service Desk	(Service Operation) The Single Point of Contact between the Service Provider and the Users. A typical Service Desk manages Incidents and Service Requests, and also handles communication with the Users.
Service Failure Analysis (SFA)	(Service Design) An Activity that identifies underlying causes of one or more IT Service interruptions. SFA identifies opportunities to improve the IT Service Provider's Processes and tools, and not just the IT Infrastructure. SFA is a time constrained, project-like activity, rather than an ongoing process of analysis. See Root Cause Analysis.
Service Hours	(Service Design) (Continual Service Improvement) An agreed time period when a particular IT Service should be Available. For example, "Monday-Friday 08:00 to 17:00 except public holidays". Service Hours should be defined in a Service Level Agreement.
Service Improvement Plan (SIP)	(Continual Service Improvement) A formal Plan to implement improvements to a Process or IT Service.
Service Knowledge Management System (SKMS)	(Service Transition) A set of tools and databases that are used to manage knowledge and information. The SKMS includes the Configuration Management System, as well as other tools and databases. The SKMS stores, manages, updates, and presents all information that an IT Service Provider needs to manage the full Lifecycle of IT Services.
Service Level	Measured and reported achievement against one or more Service Level Targets. The term Service Level is sometimes used informally to mean Service Level Target.
Service Level Agreement (SLA)	(Service Design) (Continual Service Improvement) An Agreement between an IT Service Provider and a Customer. The SLA describes the IT Service, documents Service Level Targets, and specifies the responsibilities of the IT Service Provider and the Customer. A single SLA may cover multiple IT Services or multiple Customers. See Operational Level Agreement.
Service Level Management (SLM)	(Service Design) (Continual Service Improvement) The Process responsible for negotiating Service Level Agreements, and ensuring that these are met. SLM is responsible for ensuring that all IT Service Management Processes, Operational Level Agreements, and Underpinning Contracts, are appropriate for the agreed Service Level Targets. SLM monitors and reports on Service Levels, and holds regular Customer reviews.
Service Level Package (SLP)	(Service Strategy) A defined level of Utility and Warranty for a particular Service Package. Each SLP is designed to meet the needs of a particular Pattern of Business Activity. See Line of Service.
Service Level Requirement (SLR)	(Service Design) (Continual Service Improvement) A Customer Requirement for an aspect of an IT Service. SLRs are based on Business Objectives and are used to negotiate agreed Service Level Targets.

Service Level Target	(Service Design) (Continual Service Improvement) A commitment that is documented in a Service Level Agreement. Service Level Targets are based on Service Level Requirements, and are needed to ensure that the IT Service design is Fit for Purpose. Service Level Targets should be SMART, and are usually based on KPIs.
Service Maintenance Objective	(Service Operation) The expected time that a Configuration Item will be unavailable due to planned maintenance Activity.
Service Management	Service Management is a set of specialized organizational capabilities for providing value to customers in the form of services.
Service Management Lifecycle	An approach to IT Service Management that emphasizes the importance of coordination and Control across the various Functions, Processes, and Systems necessary to manage the full Lifecycle of IT Services. The Service Management Lifecycle approach considers the Strategy, Design, Transition, Operation and Continuous Improvement of IT Services.
Service Manager	A manager who is responsible for managing the end-to-end Lifecycle of one or more IT Services. The term Service Manager is also used to mean any manager within the IT Service Provider. Most commonly used to refer to a Business Relationship Manager, a Process Manager, an Account Manager or a senior manager with responsibility for IT Services overall.
Service Operation	(Service Operation) A stage in the Lifecycle of an IT Service. Service Operation includes a number of Processes and Functions and is the title of one of the Core ITIL publications. See Operation.
Service Owner	(Continual Service Improvement) A Role which is accountable for the delivery of a specific IT Service.
Service Package	(Service Strategy) A detailed description of an IT Service that is available to be delivered to Customers. A Service Package includes a Service Level Package and one or more Core Services and Supporting Services.
Service Pipeline	(Service Strategy) A database or structured Document listing all IT Services that are under consideration or Development, but are not yet available to Customers. The Service Pipeline provides a Business view of possible future IT Services and is part of the Service Portfolio which is not normally published to Customers.
Service Portfolio	(Service Strategy) The complete set of Services that are managed by a Service Provider. The Service Portfolio is used to manage the entire Lifecycle of all Services, and includes three Categories: Service Pipeline (proposed or in Development); Service Catalogue (Live or available for Deployment); and Retired Services. See Service Portfolio Management, Contract Portfolio.
Service Portfolio Management (SPM)	(Service Strategy) The Process responsible for managing the Service Portfolio. Service Portfolio Management considers Services in terms of the Business value that they provide.

Service Potential	(Service Strategy) The total possible value of the overall Capabilities and Resources of the IT Service Provider.
Service Provider	(Service Strategy) An Organization supplying Services to one or more Internal Customers or External Customers. Service Provider is often used as an abbreviation for IT Service Provider. See Type I Service Provider, Type II Service Provider, Type III Service Provider.
Service Provider Interface (SPI)	(Service Strategy) An interface between the IT Service Provider and a User, Customer, Business Process, or a Supplier. Analysis of Service Provider Interfaces helps to coordinate end-to-end management of IT Services.
Service Provisioning Optimization (SPO)	(Service Strategy) Analyzing the finances and constraints of an IT Service to decide if alternative approaches to Service delivery might reduce Costs or improve Quality.
Service Reporting	(Continual Service Improvement) The Process responsible for producing and delivering reports of achievement and trends against Service Levels. Service Reporting should agree the format, content and frequency of reports with Customers.
Service Request	(Service Operation) A request from a User for information, or advice, or for a Standard Change or for Access to an IT Service. For example to reset a password, or to provide standard IT Services for a new User. Service Requests are usually handled by a Service Desk, and do not require an RFC to be submitted. See Request Fulfilment.
Service Sourcing	(Service Strategy) The Strategy and approach for deciding whether to provide a Service internally or to Outsource it to an External Service Provider. Service Sourcing also means the execution of this Strategy. Service Sourcing includes: • Internal Sourcing - Internal or Shared Services using Type I or Type II Service Providers. • Traditional Sourcing - Full Service Outsourcing using a Type III Service Provider. • Multivendor Sourcing - Prime, Consortium or Selective Outsourcing using Type III Service Providers.
Service Strategy	(Service Strategy) The title of one of the Core ITIL publications. Service Strategy establishes an overall Strategy for IT Services and for IT Service Management.
Service Transition	(Service Transition) A stage in the Lifecycle of an IT Service. Service Transition includes a number of Processes and Functions and is the title of one of the Core ITIL publications. See Transition.
Service Utility	(Service Strategy) The Functionality of an IT Service from the Customer's perspective. The Business value of an IT Service is created by the combination of Service Utility (what the Service does) and Service Warranty (how well it does it). See Utility.

Service Validation and Testing	(Service Transition) The Process responsible for Validation and Testing of a new or Changed IT Service. Service Validation and Testing ensures that the IT Service matches its Design Specification and will meet the needs of the Business.
Service Valuation	(Service Strategy) A measurement of the total Cost of delivering an IT Service, and the total value to the Business of that IT Service. Service Valuation is used to help the Business and the IT Service Provider agree on the value of the IT Service.
Service Warranty	(Service Strategy) Assurance that an IT Service will meet agreed Requirements. This may be a formal Agreement such as a Service Level Agreement or Contract, or may be a marketing message or brand image. The Business value of an IT Service is created by the combination of Service Utility (what the Service does) and Service Warranty (how well it does it). See Warranty.
Serviceability	(Service Design) (Continual Service Improvement) The ability of a Third Party Supplier to meet the terms of their Contract. This Contract will include agreed levels of Reliability, Maintainability or Availability for a Configuration Item.
Shift	(Service Operation) A group or team of people who carry out a specific Role for a fixed period of time. For example there could be four shifts of IT Operations Control personnel to support an IT Service that is used 24 hours a day.
Simulation modeling	(Service Design) (Continual Service Improvement) A technique that creates a detailed Model to predict the behavior of a Configuration Item or IT Service. Simulation Models can be very accurate but are expensive and time consuming to create. A Simulation Model is often created by using the actual Configuration Items that are being modeled, with artificial Workloads or Transactions. They are used in Capacity Management when accurate results are important. A simulation model is sometimes called a Performance Benchmark.
Single Point of Contact	(Service Operation) Providing a single consistent way to communicate with an Organization or Business Unit. For example, a Single Point of Contact for an IT Service Provider is usually called a Service Desk.
Single Point of Failure (SPOF)	(Service Design) Any Configuration Item that can cause an Incident when it fails, and for which a Countermeasure has not been implemented. A SPOF may be a person, or a step in a Process or Activity, as well as a Component of the IT Infrastructure. See Failure.
SLAM Chart	(Continual Service Improvement) A Service Level Agreement Monitoring Chart is used to help monitor and report achievements against Service Level Targets. A SLAM Chart is typically color coded to show whether each agreed Service Level Target has been met, missed, or nearly missed during each of the previous 12 months.
SMART	(Service Design) (Continual Service Improvement) An acronym for helping to remember that targets in Service Level Agreements and Project Plans should be Specific, Measurable, Achievable, Relevant and Timely.

Snapshot

(Service Transition) The current state of a Configuration as captured by a discovery tool.
Also used as a synonym for Benchmark.
See Baseline.

Source

See Service Sourcing.

Specification

A formal definition of Requirements. A Specification may be used to define technical or Operational Requirements, and may be internal or external.
Many public Standards consist of a Code of Practice and a Specification. The Specification defines the Standard against which an Organization can be Audited.

Stakeholder

All people who have an interest in an Organization, Project, IT Service etc. Stakeholders may be interested in the Activities, targets, Resources, or Deliverables. Stakeholders may include Customers, Partners, employees, shareholders, owners, etc.
See RACI.

Standard

A mandatory Requirement. Examples include ISO/IEC 20000 (an international Standard), an internal security Standard for Unix configuration, or a government Standard for how financial Records should be maintained. The term Standard is also used to refer to a Code of Practice or Specification published by a Standards Organization such as ISO or BSI.
See Guideline.

Standard Change

(Service Transition) A pre-approved Change that is low Risk, relatively common and follows a Procedure or Work Instruction. For example password reset or provision of standard equipment to a new employee. RFCs are not required to implement a Standard Change, and they are logged and tracked using a different mechanism, such as a Service Request.
See Change Model.

Standard Operating Procedures (SOP)

(Service Operation) Procedures used by IT Operations Management.

Standby

(Service Design) Used to refer to Resources that are not required to deliver the Live IT Services, but are available to support IT Service Continuity Plans. For example a Standby data centre may be maintained to support Hot Standby, Warm Standby or Cold Standby arrangements.

Statement of requirements (SOR)

(Service Design) A Document containing all Requirements for a product purchase, or a new or changed IT Service.
See Terms of Reference.

Status

The name of a required field in many types of Record. It shows the current stage in the Lifecycle of the associated Configuration Item, Incident, Problem etc.

Status Accounting

(Service Transition) The Activity responsible for recording and reporting the Lifecycle of each Configuration Item.

Storage Management   (Service Operation) The Process responsible for managing the storage and
                      maintenance of data throughout its Lifecycle.

Strategic   (Service Strategy) The highest of three levels of Planning and delivery (Strategic,
                      Tactical, Operational). Strategic Activities include Objective setting and long term
                      Planning to achieve the overall Vision.

Strategy   (Service Strategy) A Strategic Plan designed to achieve defined Objectives.

Super User   (Service Operation) A User who helps other Users, and assists in communication
                      with the Service Desk or other parts of the IT Service Provider. Super Users
                      typically provide support for minor Incidents and training.

Supplier   (Service Strategy) (Service Design) A Third Party responsible for supplying goods
                      or Services that are required to deliver IT services. Examples of suppliers include
                      commodity hardware and software vendors, network and telecom providers, and
                      Outsourcing Organizations.
                      See Underpinning Contract, Supply Chain.

Supplier and   (Service Design) A database or structured Document used to manage Supplier
Contract Database   Contracts throughout their Lifecycle. The SCD contains key Attributes of
(SCD)   all Contracts with Suppliers, and should be part of the Service Knowledge
                      Management System.

Supplier   (Service Design) The Process responsible for ensuring that all Contracts with
Management   Suppliers support the needs of the Business, and that all Suppliers meet their
                      contractual commitments.

Supply Chain   (Service Strategy) The Activities in a Value Chain carried out by Suppliers. A
                      Supply Chain typically involves multiple Suppliers, each adding value to the
                      product or Service.
                      See Value Network.

Support Group   (Service Operation) A group of people with technical skills. Support Groups
                      provide the Technical Support needed by all of the IT Service Management
                      Processes.
                      See Technical Management.

Support Hours   (Service Design) (Service Operation) The times or hours when support is available
                      to the Users. Typically this is the hours when the Service Desk is available. Support
                      Hours should be defined in a Service Level Agreement, and may be different from
                      Service Hours. For example, Service Hours may be 24 hours a day, but the Support
                      Hours may be 07:00 to 19:00.

Supporting Service   (Service Strategy) A Service that enables or enhances a Core Service. For example
                      a Directory Service or a Backup Service.
                      See Service Package.

SWOT Analysis	(Continual Service Improvement) A technique that reviews and analyses the internal strengths and weaknesses of an Organization and the external opportunities and threats which it faces SWOT stands for Strengths, Weaknesses, Opportunities and Threats.
System	A number of related things that work together to achieve an overall Objective. For example: • A computer System including hardware, software and Applications. • A management System, including multiple Processes that are planned and managed together. For example a Quality Management System. • A Database Management System or Operating System that includes many software modules that are designed to perform a set of related Functions.
System Management	The part of IT Service Management that focuses on the management of IT Infrastructure rather than Process.
Tactical	The middle of three levels of Planning and delivery (Strategic, Tactical, Operational). Tactical Activities include the medium term Plans required to achieve specific Objectives, typically over a period of weeks to months.
Tag	(Service Strategy) A short code used to identify a Category. For example tags EC1, EC2, EC3 etc. might be used to identify different Customer outcomes when analyzing and comparing Strategies. The term Tag is also used to refer to the Activity of assigning Tags to things.
Technical Management	(Service Operation) The Function responsible for providing technical skills in support of IT Services and management of the IT Infrastructure. Technical Management defines the Roles of Support Groups, as well as the tools, Processes and Procedures required.
Technical Observation (TO)	(Continual Service Improvement) A technique used in Service Improvement, Problem investigation and Availability Management. Technical support staff meet to monitor the behavior and Performance of an IT Service and make recommendations for improvement.
Technical Service	Synonym for Infrastructure Service.
Technical Support	Synonym for Technical Management.
Tension Metrics	(Continual Service Improvement) A set of related Metrics, in which improvements to one Metric have a negative effect on another. Tension Metrics are designed to ensure that an appropriate balance is achieved.
Terms of Reference (TOR)	(Service Design) A Document specifying the Requirements, Scope, Deliverables, Resources and schedule for a Project or Activity.
Test	(Service Transition) An Activity that verifies that a Configuration Item, IT Service, Process, etc. meets its Specification or agreed Requirements. See Service Validation and Testing, Acceptance.
Test Environment	(Service Transition) A controlled Environment used to Test Configuration Items, Builds, IT Services, Processes etc.

Third Party	A person, group, or Business who is not part of the Service Level Agreement for an IT Service, but is required to ensure successful delivery of that IT Service. For example a software Supplier, a hardware maintenance company, or a facilities department. Requirements for Third Parties are typically specified in Underpinning Contracts or Operational Level Agreements.
Third-line Support	(Service Operation) The third level in a hierarchy of Support Groups involved in the resolution of Incidents and investigation of Problems. Each level contains more specialist skills, or has more time or other Resources.
Threat	Anything that might exploit a Vulnerability. Any potential cause of an Incident can be considered to be a Threat. For example a fire is a Threat that could exploit the Vulnerability of flammable floor coverings. This term is commonly used in Information Security Management and IT Service Continuity Management, but also applies to other areas such as Problem and Availability Management.
Threshold	The value of a Metric which should cause an Alert to be generated, or management action to be taken. For example "Priority1 Incident not solved within 4 hours", "more than 5 soft disk errors in an hour", or "more than 10 failed changes in a month".
Throughput	(Service Design) A measure of the number of Transactions, or other Operations, performed in a fixed time. For example 5000 emails sent per hour, or 200 disk I/Os per second.
Total Cost of Ownership (TCO)	(Service Strategy) A methodology used to help make investment decisions. TCO assesses the full Lifecycle Cost of owning a Configuration Item, not just the initial Cost or purchase price. See Total Cost of Utilization.
Total Cost of Utilization (TCU)	(Service Strategy) A methodology used to help make investment and Service Sourcing decisions. TCU assesses the full Lifecycle Cost to the Customer of using an IT Service. See Total Cost of Ownership.
Total Quality Management (TQM)	(Continual Service Improvement) A methodology for managing continual Improvement by using a Quality Management System. TQM establishes a Culture involving all people in the Organization in a Process of continual monitoring and improvement.
Transaction	A discrete Function performed by an IT Service. For example transferring money from one bank account to another. A single Transaction may involve numerous additions, deletions and modifications of data. Either all of these complete successfully or none of them is carried out.
Transition	(Service Transition) A change in state, corresponding to a movement of an IT Service or other Configuration Item from one Lifecycle status to the next.

Transition Planning and Support	(Service Transition) The Process responsible for Planning all Service Transition Processes and co-coordinating the resources that they require. These Service Transition Processes are Change Management, Service Asset and Configuration Management, Release and Deployment Management, Service Validation and Testing, Evaluation, and Knowledge Management.
Trend Analysis	(Continual Service Improvement) Analysis of data to identify time related patterns. Trend Analysis is used in Problem Management to identify common Failures or fragile Configuration Items, and in Capacity Management as a Modeling tool to predict future behavior. It is also used as a management tool for identifying deficiencies in IT Service Management Processes.
Tuning	The Activity responsible for Planning Changes to make the most efficient use of Resources. Tuning is part of Performance Management, which also includes Performance Monitoring and implementation of the required Changes.
Type I Service Provider	(Service Strategy) An Internal Service Provider that is embedded within a Business Unit. There may be several Type I Service Providers within an Organization.
Type II Service Provider	(Service Strategy) An Internal Service Provider that provides shared IT Services to more than one Business Unit.
Type III Service Provider	(Service Strategy) A Service Provider that provides IT Services to External Customers.
Underpinning Contract (UC)	(Service Design) A Contract between an IT Service Provider and a Third Party. The Third Party provides goods or Services that support delivery of an IT Service to a Customer. The Underpinning Contract defines targets and responsibilities that are required to meet agreed Service Level Targets in an SLA.
Unit Cost	(Service Strategy) The Cost to the IT Service Provider of providing a single Component of an IT Service. For example the Cost of a single desktop PC, or of a single Transaction.
Urgency	(Service Transition) (Service Design) A measure of how long it will be until an Incident, Problem or Change has a significant Impact on the Business. For example a high Impact Incident may have low Urgency, if the Impact will not affect the Business until the end of the financial year. Impact and Urgency are used to assign Priority.
Usability	(Service Design) The ease with which an Application, product, or IT Service can be used. Usability Requirements are often included in a Statement of Requirements.
Use Case	(Service Design) A technique used to define required functionality and Objectives, and to Design Tests. Use Cases define realistic scenarios that describe interactions between Users and an IT Service or other System. See Change Case.
User	A person who uses the IT Service on a day-to-day basis. Users are distinct from Customers, as some Customers do not use the IT Service directly.

User Profile (UP)	(Service Strategy) A pattern of User demand for IT Services. Each User Profile includes one or more Patterns of Business Activity.
Utility	(Service Strategy) Functionality offered by a Product or Service to meet a particular need. Utility is often summarized as "what it does". See Service Utility.
Validation	(Service Transition) An Activity that ensures a new or changed IT Service, Process, Plan, or other Deliverable meets the needs of the Business. Validation ensures that Business Requirements are met even though these may have changed since the original Design. See Verification, Acceptance, Qualification, Service Validation and Testing.
Value Chain	(Service Strategy) A sequence of Processes that creates a product or Service that is of value to a Customer. Each step of the sequence builds on the previous steps and contributes to the overall product or Service. See Value Network.
Value for Money	An informal measure of Cost Effectiveness. Value for Money is often based on a comparison with the Cost of alternatives. See Cost Benefit Analysis.
Value Network	(Service Strategy) A complex set of Relationships between two or more groups or organizations. Value is generated through exchange of knowledge, information, goods or Services. See Value Chain, Partnership.
Value on Investment (VOI)	(Continual Service Improvement) A measurement of the expected benefit of an investment. VOI considers both financial and intangible benefits. See Return on Investment.
Variable Cost	(Service Strategy) A Cost that depends on how much the IT Service is used, how many products are produced, the number and type of Users, or something else that cannot be fixed in advance. See Variable Cost Dynamics.
Variable Cost Dynamics	(Service Strategy) A technique used to understand how overall Costs are impacted by the many complex variable elements that contribute to the provision of IT Services.
Variance	The difference between a planned value and the actual measured value. Commonly used in Financial Management, Capacity Management and Service Level Management, but could apply in any area where Plans are in place.
Verification	(Service Transition) An Activity that ensures a new or changed IT Service, Process, Plan, or other Deliverable is complete, accurate, Reliable and matches its Design Specification. See Validation, Acceptance, Service Validation and Testing.

Verification and Audit	(Service Transition) The Activities responsible for ensuring that information in the CMDB is accurate and that all Configuration Items have been identified and recorded in the CMDB. Verification includes routine checks that are part of other Processes. For example, verifying the serial number of a desktop PC when a User logs an Incident. Audit is a periodic, formal check.
Version	(Service Transition) A Version is used to identify a specific Baseline of a Configuration Item. Versions typically use a naming convention that enables the sequence or date of each Baseline to be identified. For example Payroll Application Version 3 contains updated functionality from Version 2.
Vision	A description of what the Organization intends to become in the future. A Vision is created by senior management and is used to help influence Culture and Strategic Planning.
Vital Business Function (VBF)	(Service Design) A Function of a Business Process which is critical to the success of the Business. Vital Business Functions are an important consideration of Business Continuity Management, IT Service Continuity Management and Availability Management.
Vulnerability	A weakness that could be exploited by a Threat. For example an open firewall port, a password that is never changed, or a flammable carpet. A missing Control is also considered to be a Vulnerability.
Warm Standby	Synonym for Intermediate Recovery.
Warranty	(Service Strategy) A promise or guarantee that a product or Service will meet its agreed Requirements. See Service Validation and Testing, Service Warranty.
Work in Progress (WIP)	A Status that means Activities have started but are not yet complete. It is commonly used as a Status for Incidents, Problems, Changes etc.
Work Instruction	A Document containing detailed instructions that specify exactly what steps to follow to carry out an Activity. A Work Instruction contains much more detail than a Procedure and is only created if very detailed instructions are needed.
Workaround	(Service Operation) Reducing or eliminating the Impact of an Incident or Problem for which a full Resolution is not yet available. For example by restarting a failed Configuration Item. Workarounds for Problems are documented in Known Error Records. Workarounds for Incidents that do not have associated Problem Records are documented in the Incident Record.
Workload	The Resources required to deliver an identifiable part of an IT Service. Workloads may be Categorized by Users, groups of Users, or Functions within the IT Service. This is used to assist in analyzing and managing the Capacity, Performance and Utilization of Configuration Items and IT Services. The term Workload is sometimes used as a synonym for Throughput.

References

Bon, J. van (ed.) (2007). *Foundations of IT Service Management - based on ITIL V3.* Zaltbommel: Van Haren Publishing

Office of Government Commerce (2007). *ITIL: Service Strategy.* London: The Stationary Office.

Office of Government Commerce (2007). *Glossary ITIL Version 3*: http://www.best-management-practice.com

Index

ITIL Books
The Official Books from itSMF

Foundations of IT Service Management Based on ITIL®V3
Now updated to encompass all of the implications of the V3 refresh of ITIL, the new V3 Foundations book looks at Best Practices, focusing on the Lifecycle approach, and covering the ITIL Service Lifecycle, processes and functions for Service Strategy, Service Design, Service Operation, Service Transition and Continual Service Improvement.
ISBN: 978 908753057 0 (ENGLISH EDITION)
PRICE €39.95 EXCL TAX

Foundations of IT Service Management Based on ITIL®
The bestselling ITIL® V2 edition of this popular guide is available as usual, with 13 language options to give you the widest possible global perspective on this important subject.
ISBN: 978 907721258 5 (ENGLISH EDITION)
PRICE €39.95 EXCL TAX

IT Service Management Based on ITIL®V3: A Pocket Guide
A concise summary for ITIL®V3, providing a quick and portable reference tool to this leading set of best practices for IT Service Management.
ISBN: 978 908753102 7 (ENGLISH EDITION)
PRICE €14.95 EXCL TAX

ISO/IEC 20000
The Official Books from itSMF

ISO/IEC 20000: An Introduction
Promoting awareness of the certification for organizations within the IT Service Management environment.
ISBN: 978 908753081 5 (ENGLISH EDITION)
PRICE €49.95 EXCL TAX

Implementing ISO/IEC 20000 Certification: The Roadmap
Practical advice, to assist readers through the requirements of the standard, the scoping, the project approach, the certification procedure and management of the certification.
ISBN: 978 908753082 2
PRICE €39.95 EXCL TAX

ISO/IEC 20000: A Pocket Guide
A quick and accessible guide to the fundamental requirements for corporate certification.
ISBN: 978 907721279 0 (ENGLISH EDITION)
PRICE €14.95 EXCL TAX

Other leading ITSM Books from itSMF

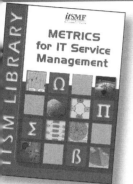

Metrics for IT Service Management

A general guide to the use of metrics as a mechanism to control and steer IT service organizations, with consideration of the design and implementation of metrics in service organizations using industry standard frameworks.

ISBN: 978 907721269 1
PRICE €39.95 EXCL TAX

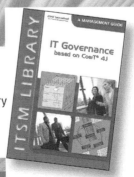

Six Sigma for IT Management

The first book to provide a coherent view and guidance for using the Six Sigma approach successfully in IT Service Management, whilst aiming to merge both Six Sigma and ITIL® into a single unified approach to continuous improvement. Six Sigma for IT Management: A Pocket Guide is also available.

ISBN: 978 907721230 1 (ENGLISH EDITION)
PRICE €39.95 EXCL TAX

Frameworks for IT Management

An unparalleled guide to the myriad of IT management instruments currently available to IT and business managers. Frameworks for IT Management: A Pocket Guide is also available.

ISBN: 978 907721290 5 (ENGLISH EDITION)
PRICE €39.95 EXCL TAX

IT Governance based on CobiT 4.1:
A Management Guide

Detailed information on the overall process model as well as the theory behind it.

ISBN: 978 90 8753116 4 (ENGLISH EDITION)
PRICE €20,75 EXCL TAX

Printed in Great Britain
by Amazon.co.uk, Ltd.,
Marston Gate.